Write Your
Life Story

The Daily Telegraph

Write Your Life Story

HOW TO RECORD AND PRESENT YOUR MEMORIES FOR FAMILY AND FRIENDS TO ENJOY

THIRD EDITION

MICHAEL OKE

howtobooks

Published by How To Books Ltd,
Spring Hill House, Spring Hill Road,
Begbroke, Oxford OX5 1RX, United Kingdom.
Tel: (01865) 375794. Fax: (01865) 379162.
info@howtobooks.co.uk
www.howtobooks.co.uk

ISBN 978 1 84528 305 6

First edition 2001
Reprinted 2002
Reprinted 2003 (twice)
Revised edition 2006
Third edition 2008

British Library Cataloguing in Publication Data.
A catalogue record for this book is available from
the British Library.

Cover design by Baseline Arts Ltd, Oxford
Produced for How To Books by Deer Park Productions
Typeset by Pantek Arts Ltd, Maidstone, Kent.
Printed and bound by Cromwell Press, Trowbridge, Wiltshire

NOTE: The material contained in this book is set out in good faith for general guidance and no
liability can be accepted for loss or expense incurred as a result of relying in particular
circumstances on statements made in the book. Laws and regulations are complex and liable
to change, and readers should check the current position with the relevant authorities before
making personal arrangements.

Contents

Foreword

Long ago I had a Granny and a Grandma. They were both white-haired gentle women.

Granny, the Scottish one, liked to read Westerns as she rocked in her chair and sucked on a toffee. Grandma once ran a stall at Newbiggin beach in the North-East, and chaired meetings using an olivewood gavel.

I'd like to tell you more, but I know hardly anything else about them. I will never know what songs they sang as they washed up, which flowers they loved, or what views they held.

When they died, effectively, for me, they disappeared without trace. There were old photographs but in this context they are hardly worth a thousand words.

If only they had left a written account of their lives . . .

I believe that one of the greatest gifts we can give to our families, and bequeath to those who follow us, is an intimate, first-hand account of our lives.

This book will make the task of capturing you and your life enjoyable for you, and enriching for those who read it. Mike Oke feels passionately that everyone has within them a marvellous story – the tale of their life. He's just the man to help you tell it.

Neil Patrick
Former Editor-in-Chief
Yours magazine

Acknowledgements

My initial thanks, as always, go to those without whom this book would not have been possible: the scores of people – friends – I have had the privilege of assisting with their own precious life stories over the past 17 years. My thanks go to them, especially those who have directly contributed to this book.

Special thanks are due to my wonderful wife Mychelle, my constant support and friend, for putting up with all my hare-brained ideas, usually in the small hours of the morning, and for believing so whole-heartedly in me. Katie and Matthew are the shining lights in our life – they can never know how much they are loved.

The team at Bound Biographies are due my thanks for believing in our work and for putting up with me. Tony warrants a particular mention for all his help, not least with this book.

Since writing the last edition an event has happened to bring home to me the importance of writing life stories. I have lectured about the value of this for years, but it was only with the death of my own dear mother in October 2007 that I truly appreciated what a written record means... or the lack of it. It is now my aim to ensure that Mum lives on through the writing of her darling husband, Michael, after whom I am named, and the other children, Anita, Marie and Budge.

This book is dedicated to the memory of a very special lady, Marie Beryl Oke.

Introduction

This book bears little resemblance to the first edition of *Write Your Life Story* published in 2001. So much has changed in seven short years… perhaps emphasising just how much happens in a life of ten times that duration.

The book has more than doubled in size, with the addition of a substantial memory jogging appendix as well as a second one in which can be written a few of your 'favourite things' to set the ball rolling in the writing of your own life story. Further updates have been provided in this new edition.

Since *Who Do You Think You Are?* came to our screens in 2004, the world of genealogy has not been the same. The twin phenomenon of the 'Paxman effect' and access to online census returns has led to an insatiable appetite for family history. Who would have thought that so genteel a hobby could have brought tears to the eyes of a man who eats politicians for breakfast! The nation was gripped and has been ever since.

This new edition of *Write Your Life Story* offers even more tips for the enthusiastic hobbyist looking to record some of the incredible years witnessed within living memory and special people and events encountered along the way. Whilst the final record will be a treasure trove for loved-ones, it is the intention of this book to make the writing journey equally rewarding.

It is hoped that this book, along with the companion volume, *Times of Our Lives*, which follows a typical life of someone born in Britain during the 1930s, '40s or '50s, is the definitive aid for those considering writing their life story.

Give it a go. You'll be glad you did… and so will those fortunate enough to read it.

Michael Oke

Why Write Your Life Story?

1

Knowing why you want to write your life story will influence what is included. This chapter will look at reasons for writing, as well as, hopefully, providing inspiration for those not yet convinced of the validity of such a project.

Knowing why you want to write

There are many reasons to write and it is likely that at least one of the following will strike a chord.

Nursing a desire to write

Maybe you have never had the time, or possibly the confidence, to start writing until now. Alternatively, you may have kept a diary all your life and now want it collated and edited into a book. This is your opportunity.

Case study – Dorothy's ambition realised

Dorothy had always harboured a desire to write. As a child she was forever sending snippets to the *Yorkshire Evening Post* for inclusion in Uncle Mac's column – some even being accepted. Sadly, her mother did not share Dorothy's enthusiasm, and whenever she caught her with a pencil in her hand, would tell her to 'Do something useful – go and help Dad in the garden.'

Looking after a husband and four active children meant that, in her middle years, Dorothy never had the time to write, but after John died she took the opportunity to sit down and write a tribute to him. Initially she recalled the special times they had together, but then she started to write about her childhood and of the years bringing up her own children. It was a proud day when Dorothy's lifelong ambition of writing a book was realised... *The Gospel According to John's Wife*.

Remembering parents or grandparents

How many times do we look at boxes of old photographs and wish we knew something about the faces before us? There may not even be any names on the back to identify the people.

As time passes so there are fewer people who have memories of those from a previous generation. You might be the only person who still remembers your grandparents. If you do not record what you know of their lives these precious details will be lost forever.

Interestingly, as you write about your parents and grand-parents, you may well spot patterns which you and perhaps your children have repeated.

Responding to a request to write

This might be by a family member, perhaps a child, grand-child, nephew or niece, or maybe a friend has been nagging at you to put pen to paper.

It is now part of the National Curriculum to seek 'eyewitness accounts', so perhaps a neighbour's child has sown the seed for this autobiographical adventure.

Biographies are the most popular form of reading ... they are even more interesting when they are about someone you know.

Q: I've never written anything longer than a note to the milkman. How am I going to write a book?

A: If you can write a letter, you really can write a book. Break it down into bite-sized chunks and just write the way you speak. If the book is intended for people who know and love you, they are on your side already. They are not going to say, 'I loved the book, but there was a split infinitive on page 72 that ruined the whole thing for me.' They love you for being you, and if you write the way you speak, your character will shine out from every page.

You can always have the writing typed up and edited afterwards, if required, but start by getting your precious memories down on paper – all the rest can come later.

If you have been writing letters all your life, you will know how to express yourself; a book is just like writing a series of letters.

Remembering your spouse or loved one
Writing about a lost partner or loved one can be a cathartic experience, although sometimes a period of time has to elapse before you feel ready to embark on such a project. What you write can be a wonderful tribute to a person very dear to your heart.

Providing a record for future generations
Maybe the initiative has come from within to leave something for your grandchildren, your godchildren or future

generations, possibly even as a surprise gift. Perhaps you wish that you had been left such a record by your forebears.

The world has changed phenomenally over the past few decades. Someone in their seventies or eighties has probably witnessed more change in their lifetime than in any other period of history, and even a 50-year-old will remember a time before decimalisation, the unification of Germany, England winning the World Cup, using slide rules and receiving free school milk. Then there's the first time you tasted foreign food or perhaps the luxury of going abroad on holiday. All these memories and many more will provide a fascinating record of the twentieth century for future generations.

Case study – Celebrating Sid's life

Sid and Mary decided to write a joint book. They felt it best not to confer, and while they knew that they would undoubtedly cover some of the same material, it would be interesting to read of events from a different viewpoint.

Sid had just written about their wedding day when he became ill. Sadly, Sid deteriorated rapidly and died within six weeks.

It was several months before Mary was able to contemplate writing again. Many tears were shed as she read what Sid had written, but she resolved to continue – she even decided to include a few of the many tributes received from friends when Sid died.

The project became a celebration of Sid and Mary's life together, and it was a great source of comfort for Mary to know that Sid would live on through the book. The final volume was presented to the family on what would have been Sid's 80th birthday.

Recording a particular period of your life

You may have served in a war in some capacity, either seeing action or supporting the war effort indirectly. There again, you may have been evacuated or remember the hardships of rationing, or perhaps you never had it so good growing up in the 1960s.

Alternatively, you may have had a particularly interesting childhood being brought up abroad. Perhaps you had an extended stay in hospital, or nursed a loved one through a lengthy illness at home. Such subjects make for fascinating reading, and, who knows, once you've caught the writing bug you may want to record other parts of your life.

Being inspired by a TV programme

Watching television has a way of opening up so many memories, especially programmes like *Dad's Army* or *Foyle's War*, if they are set during a formative period of our lives. The sights, sounds, values and events can all help to relive those years. For others, *The Good Life* or *Only Fools and Horses* may be nostalgic as we see mobile phones the size of bricks, and fashions and styles we now cringe at but which we were quite happy to adopt ourselves during those years.

There are also those programmes which follow volunteers through experiences with which we might be familiar, be they National Service, schooldays in the 1950s, or perhaps *The 1940s House*. Such programmes may have set you thinking about the times before electric washing machines and refrigerators. You can describe how washday was such a chore for your mother (or even yourself), and how it was doubly difficult in wet weather as the Dutch airer and clothes horse had to be used... no tumble dryers or radiators to help in those days. Then there was *Reckitt's blue*, *Robin starch*, mangles, the copper...

The BBC programme *Who Do You Think You Are?* has also inspired many to review their immediate ancestors. Recording these details about the family and continuing with your own life story may be your impetus for wanting to write – if so, advice is provided in the next chapter.

Illustrating how the workplace has changed

Many jobs are almost unrecognisable compared with thirty or forty years ago when modern technology meant a comptometer for the book-keeper. You also probably had to clock in, losing a quarter of an hour's pay if you were so much as three minutes late.

There was an obvious hierarchy, this often being defined by the hat that was worn, be it flat cap, trilby or bowler. There was also the associated respect: the boss was 'Mr Tilbury' – no one would have called him 'Martin' ... and, yes, the bosses were invariably men. In fact, women often had to resign when they got married!

A six-day working week was commonplace. If you were lucky perhaps you only worked Saturday mornings, leaving Saturday afternoon for shopping; there was no late night opening, and Sunday trading was inconceivable. And how many weeks holiday did you get – one or two?

Your nursing days may have been a fantastic time and you want to record how things have changed so dramatically in the medical profession. You might remember waxing the floor, or perhaps how penicillin was the wonder drug after the days of M&B 693 and 760. Perhaps you pre-date the NHS, or witnessed its infancy.

Perhaps you served an apprenticeship, with your father having to sign the indenture because you were under 21 – he might even have had to pay for the privilege of your articles if you were taken on in a profession like accountancy!

Writing a company book

You may have started a business and want to record its history, perhaps weaving chapters within your own life story. Looking at the company now, who would have believed that on one occasion you had to sell the typewriter to pay the wages?

Or perhaps you worked for one company throughout your career when a job was for life. After five years you might barely have progressed from making the tea, whereas today you are likely to be the longest-serving employee!

Writing your story is a way of recording the social tapestry of life in the workplace in the second half of the twentieth century. You might like to send a copy of your book, or at least the relevant chapters, to the company for their archives, or lodge a copy with the local library where it will be a valuable record for social historians in years to come.

Looking for a hobby

If you are looking for a hobby to exercise your mind, writing your life story is the perfect choice. It can be as gentle or demanding as you require, depending on whether you write purely from memory or decide to undertake more extensive research. The latter may involve visiting relatives to pick their brains, referring to some of the excellent books and videos widely available, or visiting a few of the many nostalgia museums.

Q: Don't I have to be really old before I write my life story?

A: No, just because you write your autobiography does not mean that there won't be more chapters to come. Many people write in their fifties and early sixties, some younger still.

Often the desire is sparked by a life change like retirement (or early retirement), or because the time is right to realise that ambition of writing a book. Writing about your life thus far helps to draw a line under what has gone before, allowing you to move on to your next adventure. Since completing her book, one author went trekking in China.

If you write a book in your fifties, there's nothing to stop you writing a sequel in your eighties!

Writing for yourself

Sadly, all too often people find it difficult to say, 'I am writing my life story because I want to.'

You are interesting and unique. You have insights, feelings and thoughts that you will find both stimulating and enjoyable to reflect upon and express. You will open up many wonderful memories and also be amazed at what you learn about yourself in the process.

You may have something interesting you want to say ... or maybe it's your soapbox. Either way, you're entitled to it. Don't apologise, just enjoy the experience and celebrate your life.

Writing your autobiography is immense fun, all the more so if the process is shared – this will be considered in the next chapter.

Q: I want to write, but I have never been any good at spelling and grammar. Does it matter?

A: Please don't be deflected in your enthusiasm for writing by such fears . . . and don't use them as an excuse for not writing. The important thing is to get your story down on paper first.

You can play around with the manuscript later if you want to – plenty of help and technology is available. Suggestions regarding consistency and editing the manuscript can be found in Chapter 12.

Thinking about Granny

If you are still in doubt as to whether to write, consider how you would feel if someone special had given you a copy of their life story – your grandmother, a parent, your favourite uncle or an inspirational teacher. Imagine reading about their parents, their childhood, their successes and aspirations… and possibly even their feelings about you on the day you were born.

Such a treasure trove is likely to be one of the few things you would rescue if your house was burning down. If you would cherish such a possession, isn't it likely that your loved ones would too?

Receiving this book as a present

You have made a start simply by reading this far. Hopefully you will feel inspired to read on … and maybe even to put pen to paper.

Changing horses mid-stream

It doesn't matter if your reasons for writing change during the project. You might set out with the intention of writing to remember your parents, yet find yourself engrossed in your early career, or intend to write solely about your childhood but find yourself writing about the Millennium. The more you write, the better, and you can always adjust the Introduction to account for your change of heart – after all, in writing your life story, the most difficult person to seek approval from is yourself!

Areas of caution

Two further reasons for writing are considered below. However, great care must be exercised before embarking on a book with these motives in mind.

Writing to set the record straight

It might be that you have felt misunderstood, or perhaps a book has been written which tells the story differently from how you remember it. Writing to set the record straight may not necessarily be a negative focus, but if it is, great care has to be taken not to offend. The law of libel is fierce and any litigation can be financially ruinous. At best you might lose friends, at worst you might also be rendered penniless.

Think carefully before putting anything contentious into print. This book is intended for those seeking to write gentle family memoirs, not blockbusters aiming to bring down governments. If that is your intention, you should seek advice elsewhere.

Seeking fame and fortune

Unless you are one of the very few individuals who receive an advance from a publisher for a manuscript yet to be written, no guarantees can ever be made about making money from writing your memoirs. Indeed, if such an advance is forthcoming, it is likely that you are already in the 'fame and fortune' category.

Please think very carefully before you put pen to paper if your motive is financial. Apart from the well-publicised exceptions, very few 'unknown' people make money from their autobiography. Publishing is a notoriously fickle industry and this book makes no promises in the realms of publication.

Beware, there is an industry known as vanity publishing which will be discussed later. The advice here is to keep your eyes open and your chequebook closed.

As long as your reasons for writing are wholesome, you will experience a great sense of achievement and satisfaction once you have finished.

Dealing with modesty

Modesty is the biggest single reason why people do not write their life stories. We are taught to be humble and self-effacing.

Despite this, we all know someone who should write an auto-biography: the lady down the road who brought up seven children and adopted three more during the war, and the kindly octogenarian at church who has seen so much change in his lifetime. They should write their life stories ... but me? Oh no!

Even within the family there are those we wish had written something:

> 'Great Aunt Ethel was such a character; if only we had put the tape recorder on when she was telling us about her amazing childhood. She remembered having gas installed, and even then it was only downstairs because the pipes were charged for by the yard and her parents could not afford to have them fitted upstairs. She was given a candle when she went to bed, and so expert was her mother at cutting this to size that if Aunt Ethel was only to read for ten minutes, the candle would extinguish virtually to the second after the tenth minute had elapsed. But there are so many stories which have been forgotten.'

Q: Isn't it big-headed to write about myself?

A: If this is your concern, the odds are that you are not big-headed.

If you were given a book written by your grandfather, you would be mesmerised from cover to cover. You certainly would not accuse him of being big-headed; you would simply be delighted that he had left some of those cherished memories for posterity.

Just because you write your life story does not mean that you are being immodest. Indeed, if you are concerned about such issues in the first place, it tends to imply that you are modest by nature, as will be evident in your writing. Just keep your story simple and write the way you speak, and you will be assured of a fascinating record for friends and family to enjoy.

Listening to the experts

Set out below are some comments from those who have written their autobiographies and who have been kind enough to take the time to share what was the inspiration behind their writing:

Family life has always been very important to me. Coming from a very large and loving family has left me with many memories. A few years ago it became an obsession for me to write all these memories down for my family and future generations.

Writing my book led to many interesting events. Numerous relatives and friends have asked to read it with amazing reactions. Through this I have found out so much more about my ancestors and even met relatives I never knew existed. It has made so much difference to my life.

Mrs Brandon, Hertfordshire

We have three lovely daughters and decided to give them an early legacy of a beautiful leather-bound book of the family's memoirs. We found it great fun compiling our days of yesteryear, recalling all those little incidents, anecdotes, happy and even sad days which creep into one's lives.

We had immense pleasure in presenting our girls with a signed copy on Gordon's 70th birthday, and truly hope it will inspire them to continue with the next generation.

Mr & Mrs Boorman, Kent

My book was the compilation of diaries and photographs kept over thirty-three years when my husband and I bought a plot of land, designed and built a bungalow for ourselves.

Mrs Simpson, Gloucestershire

I had the experience of reading some of my father's war memoirs and his early life (written in an exercise book) and found it so fascinating that I felt I must pass on to my children, grandchildren and future descendants something of my life. My dad had not completed his work when he died.

Mrs Dudley, Hampshire

Jottings hoarded over many years were lying in a file intended to be rewritten sometime. All the notes were related to my years working as a nurse. Changes over the last fifty years merited record. Retirement and re-marriage meant moving house. Decision time had arrived ... the file came too. A friend offered to help me collate the material and the book was conceived in earnest.

Mrs Mortimer, Morayshire

I wrote my story mainly for my own benefit. I had been pondering the idea for several years, as I had a lot of thoughts churning over in my head that I didn't want to talk about. One evening, late at night, I found an old exercise book and started jotting little notes down. I wrote most evenings, not because I had to, but because I really wanted to. It all seemed to flow – there was so much to write about.

Mrs Davies, Hampshire

As far back as I can remember, and that is quite some time, I always admired and can still see a photograph on my mother's lounge table of her three brothers all dressed in Scottish uniform ... but being so young I never appreciated their loss in the Great War and Mother never mentioned their fate. I felt I must write something about what I knew of my family background to ensure that future generations were not equally in the dark.

Mr Blake, Devon

I wrote letters home during my 27 years in the Navy. When my mother died I was amazed to find them and read them avidly. I put them into a book – they make a fascinating social record.

Mr Sherwood, Kent

I kept the whole project a secret from my daughters, who were both surprised and delighted when they were presented with the book. We seldom ask our parents about their early lives, and as we become older most of us have regrets we did not do so. Hopefully I have filled in some of this information for my offspring and the grandchildren, who find life as it was for their grandmother quite unbelievable.

Mrs Long, Cheshire

After a long illness, I felt very depressed; I'd no interest in life or people. I was a misery. Unable to sleep one night, I read a magazine and saw an article on how to write your life story. Ha! What story would my life make? I'm in a wheelchair, can only go out when I'm taken. Then I found myself thinking back.

Picking up pen and paper, I began to write about the good times in my life, places I'd been, people I've known over the years, my greenhouse and lovely garden, the little dogs I've had, the hard but happy experiences of my nursing life. The more I opened my memory box, the more I remembered.

My writing has opened a new chapter in my life. Looking at old photos and reading old diaries is fun. They take you back in years. I am now writing my second book, and am too busy to be a misery… (and I will be 90 next birthday).

Mrs Crampton, Goole

Checklist

-    Why do you want to write your life story?
-    What excites you most about the prospect of writing?
-    If your grandfather had written his life story, what details would you want him to have included? Often the smallest details are the most fascinating. If my grandfather wrote that he cleaned his shoes every night, the fact that he felt

it worthy of inclusion is good enough for me ... it also explains why Dad was so paranoid about me cleaning my cricket boots! These are the details you should consider including in your manuscript.

Assignments

- Write down your reasons for writing your life story. Don't worry if these change during the course of the project.
- Your book will be around long after you have gone and may well be read by people who never met you. Consider what you might write about yourself that will convey to such people the sort of person you are.
- If you are still unsure as to whether to embark on this project, write down your reservations and discuss them with a friend.

Thinking Things Through 2

There are many ways to record your life story and this chapter will help you decide what sort of project you might like to undertake.

Before proceeding further it is worth considering four factors:

- ✒ your audience
- ✒ what type of record you want
- ✒ whether you require any assistance
- ✒ your proposed style of writing.

Knowing your audience

It is important that you are aware of your readership because the book will be shaped accordingly. For example, if your son has asked you to write you may consider it unnecessary to describe life in the East End of London after the war – after all, he was brought up there. However, not only will your view-points differ, even of the same event, but assumptions you make for him will not hold for every reader. What happens when a grandchild or a neighbour asks to read the book?

Such comparisons become even more stark if you have lived abroad. For those who know little or nothing about Colonial East Africa, wartime France or Carnaby Street in the 1960s, an opportunity will have been lost to provide a fascinating read.

Thinking laterally

Once you have decided to embark on writing a book, it is worth thinking more widely. As memories of your childhood become ever more remote, so new generations will find it increasingly difficult to understand a secret language ... who will know what ten bob was in thirty years' time?

For the purposes of your life story it is best to assume little prior knowledge – or even none – so as to appeal to a wider audience. You can still include the family in-jokes, most of which will probably go unnoticed by the uninitiated. Where such references come across as a little odd, you may need to include a small explanation for those not 'in the know'.

Being diplomatic

For the sake of diplomacy it is also worth considering who might potentially read your book. If a close friend had written an autobiography you would undoubtedly be keen to find out if you were mentioned. The same will be true of those who read your book. The fact that you have sent someone a Christmas card for the last 43 years must mean something. Just a mention of their name and perhaps a sentence or two could save a lot of awkwardness if, and when, they come to read the book.

A simple way to deal with this is to review your Christmas card list and address books, and make a list of who should be included in your book. Invariably an anecdote or two will spring to mind, which can then be incorporated at the appropriate point in your writing.

While it may be your intention that the book will only be read by the grandchildren, you will be amazed by how many people ask to read it when they know that they have an author in their midst.

Deciding what type of record you want

There are many ways to record the story of your life and being aware of the possibilities may lead to a more fulfilling, enjoyable and comprehensive project.

The labels themselves are not particularly important, especially as many of them become blurred. What does matter is that you know what type of record you want to achieve.

For convenience, the terms 'life story', 'biography' and 'autobiography' will be used interchangeably in this book, although the information will invariably apply to whatever project you decide to embark upon.

Here are some of your options:

Autobiography
This is the most common term used if you write your life story, and, by definition, is written by the subject of the book.

Alternative structures are suggested in Chapter 5, but usually an autobiography will flow chronologically, beginning with what the author knows of his or her immediate ancestors. The author is then introduced and the account of his or her life follows.

Joint autobiography
This may sound like a contradiction but is, in fact, a very popular way of presenting the life stories of two or more people – usually a married couple. Each partner writes an account

that either stands side by side or is woven into the book. Assuming that both partners are equally enthusiastic, this can be an immensely enjoyable project.

Another variation is for one partner to undertake the majority of the writing, while the other provides the occasional few pages.

Several sample frameworks for such projects can be found in Chapter 5.

Biography

Such a book is written by a third party (or ghostwriter) either with or without the permission of the subject. The lives of the famous are often ghostwritten, and even books claiming to be autobiographies are often written 'with assistance'. The quality of these varies enormously.

There is nothing wrong with ghostwritten books, but it is rare to find one that fully encapsulates the character of the subject. We tend to write the way we speak and our own book will reflect this. Our character and mannerisms will shine through, something which is very hard for anyone else to capture.

The term 'biography' is often used generically to refer to the diverse area of life story and reminiscence, including autobiography.

Joint biography

This is where more than one third party writes about the subject of the book.

Some people ask their children to write an account of childhood to be included either in the main body of the book or as an appendix. Again, sample frameworks for such projects can be found in Chapter 5.

Memoir

Sometimes used interchangeably with the words 'biography' and 'autobiography', a memoir tends to be a collection of anecdotes rather than a detailed chronological history.

You may remember little about your childhood, or do not want to write about it for one reason or another, but hopefully that will not deflect you from writing snippets about the rest of your life. Characters you have known, stories from your national service days, anecdotes from your career, hobbies, parenthood and dozens of other subjects all make for an excellent memoir.

Q: I only want to write about my childhood, but I have a few articles and some poetry – is it worth doing?

A: The project is well worth undertaking simply for the satisfaction that you will derive from it, quite apart from the joy it will give to others close to you. The information contained within this book applies whether you are writing about a small part of your life or all of it. Additionally, suggestions as to how you might present poetry, letters, articles, documents, etc. can be found in Chapter 13. Your intended project is just as valid as any other.

Diary or journal

This is probably the purest and most intimate form of autobiography. You may have been keeping a diary for years, or have just begun. Whether this is kept as a private record or is made public, and if so in what detail, is entirely up to you. However, if you are of a particularly candid disposition and are outspoken in your opinions, the reference to libel in Chapter 11 might best be borne in mind. What you write in private may need some editing before it is suitable for a wider readership.

Family history

While this sounds imposing, it can be an autobiography with a stronger emphasis on the wider family than might otherwise be the case. In its more formal guise, the family history can be a well-researched and thorough document with leanings towards genealogy.

Q: Do I have to include the dates of all my ancestors?

A: If there are only a few it does no harm, but if your grand-mother was one of 13 it could get a little tedious. The important detail is that she, with her twin sister Mabel (born three minutes earlier the other side of midnight), was one of 13 born over a span of 16 years from 1895. The twins were born in 1904, had three older brothers and two older sisters, and there was another set of twins later – Arthur and Betty. Your favourite was Aunt Tootles (Winifred – don't know why she was called Tootles!). Also, in his final years Uncle Frank lived with you, with that infernal dog of his called Norman. You know nothing of the others.

If you have all the dates of birth you may as well use them – they will be particularly useful for any genealogist in the family. However, to stop the narrative becoming tedious you could list the dates in a table, include them in an appendix or produce a family tree.

Genealogy

Genealogical research is pursued with great dedication by many amateur and professional enthusiasts. As plenty of guidance is readily available elsewhere, research methods will not be discussed here.

The findings of such research can fit easily within the frame-work of a family book, although care has to be taken not to create an imbalance. With this in mind, lists of raw data and census returns might better be encompassed within an appendix unless the book is a pure genealogical record.

Guidance about presenting and including family trees within your own book can be found in Chapter 13, 'Presentation' and Chapter 17, 'Producing Your Own Book Part 2 – Technical Considerations.'

Sticking to what you know

This book focuses primarily upon living memories – what we recall and what is readily to hand rather than any detailed research. A chat with Great Aunt Maud may well provide a treasure trove of stories about Grandma's childhood. Documents will still be available in public record offices long after Great Aunt Maud and her precious memories are gone.

Case study – Grandpa becomes side-tracked

Isabelle, Joseph and James asked Grandpa to write a few memories for them about his schooldays. Grandpa had often pointed out his old school as they had passed in the car – there had only been two classes and the school had long since been converted into a house. They also wanted to hear more about what he remembered of his parents and the mischief he'd got up to.

Grandpa took the view that a job worth doing was worth doing well and attacked the project with gusto. After he had been to a few museums and devoured several excellent reference books, Grandpa decided that before he put pen to paper he would do a bit of research into his ancestry. He was soon bitten by the genealogy bug and wanted to go back further and further. Each time he thought he was getting to the point where he would start his own writing, a new line of enquiry emerged and off he went.

Isabelle, Joseph and James will inherit files full of census returns and dates and names of distant ancestors dating back to the eighteenth century, and no doubt much earlier if Grandpa has his way. Sadly, they still know no more about their great-grandparents, Grandpa's school and the mischief he got up to as a lad.

Novel

It is well recognised that most first novels are heavily autobiographical. It stands to reason that we write about what we know best and draw from experience.

Be careful if this is your preferred presentation; thinly disguised characterisations can cause ill-feeling by those who suspect they are the subjects ... not least because it is difficult to separate fact from fiction.

Pictorial presentation

For those with extensive collections of photographs and other templates and with little desire to write extensively, a pictorial presentation of your life is a sound option. This can be presented in a photograph album or other special volume. Alternatively, sophisticated reproduction methods allow for copies to be produced in a cost-effective manner. Further details can be found in Chapter 13.

Obviously, any information you have about the pictures will be a great bonus, and, who knows, it might encourage you to take the plunge and write your life story.

Collaborative ventures

In all the above, apart from perhaps the diary, it is possible for others to contribute to the book. This will usually be your partner, but there is no reason why it should not be a sibling, a cousin, or even a child or grandchild ... a whole family celebration.

Case study – Including the whole family

While sorting through some family archives, Julia found a diary written by her father during the Great War. She knew he had written one, but had never seen it. Julia was mesmerised as she read about her father's time in the Camel Corps in Egypt and wanted to reproduce his diary for the family.

Case study – Including the whole family cont...

Knowing that there was not enough material for a book, Julia decided to write about her childhood and early life before she was married. She was able to encourage her two children to do the same, and even the five grandchildren wrote a couple of pages each. A few pictures and a leather binding enhanced the overall presentation and now *Four Generations of the Lloyd Family* resides in pride of place on Julia's bookcase.

Being aware of opportunities offered by technology

While this book will primarily concentrate on the written record and presentation in book-form, this is not your only option. A sound archive can be considered, which has the benefit of preserving voices, with all their inherent character, for posterity.

Recording can be undertaken in isolation, but there is nothing wrong with someone asking you questions and their voice also being heard. In either case, preparatory notes on the topics to be covered will help.

Tapes can later be transcribed and printed by a friend or a local secretarial service to form the basis of a book if that is your desire. Of course, the reverse is also true: having written your life story, you might also enjoy reading it onto tape.

Using video or DVD takes this idea a step further, and for those with a flair for technology, there is nothing to stop you setting up your own website on the Internet with regular updates. The possibilities are endless.

Who Do You Think You Are?

This excellent BBC television series follows well-known people as they research their family history. Genealogy can be perceived as dry and dull, a list of dates and names, but the success of this programme has been to bring history to life. Who can forget Jeremy Paxman sitting tearfully in the cramped Glasgow tenement where his widowed great-grand-mother, Mary McKay, lived with nine children. Her choice was that or the workhouse... and the workhouse would have meant losing her children.

The power of such scenes, coupled with online census returns, has introduced a whole new audience to the delights of genealogy and family history.

Another of the programme's assets has been the use of historians to provide background information, describing conditions and expectations of people in particular industries, different walks of life, various parts of the country or even further afield. For anyone looking to write a family history, such details are invaluable, helping the reader to gain a wider appreciation of those they are reading about.

Creating Empathy

Once the background information has been gathered, a useful device is to ask what that person would have felt. What would have led to such a decision, and what - if any - options were available to them? Such conjecture might stimulate a desire in the reader to discover more, so furthering the research.

Further Resources

There are genealogy exhibitions and family history fairs aplenty, providing an amazing array of resources and memorabilia from maps and medals to clever bits of technology.

When it comes to the internet, quite apart from the invaluable census returns, the information available is vast and increasing exponentially. Additionally, numerous websites provide access to even further information, although many of these incur fees.

Professional research services are also available, but one of the delights of the internet is the free help offered by amateur enthusiasts. The internet has spawned an army of thousands willing to share their findings. Such generous-hearted people have always existed, but the internet has united them to provide a phenomenal resource.

Note of Caution

Historians are never happier than when sharing their knowledge with an enthusiastic listener, and amateur genealogists are similarly generous in sharing findings with fellow devotees. However, don't expect the doors of libraries, public record offices and churches to open magically as they do to the likes of Messrs Paxman, Fry and co. The BBC has much more clout than you or I when it comes to eliciting help. We are much more likely to be guided to the relevant section of the archive and left to get on with it!

The Golden Rule

With an infinite amount of information available, if you are looking to record a family history it is important not to get sidetracked. Your findings need to be catalogued and recorded, then presented in a meaningful, digestible manner, a book being the perfect medium. The danger of leaving files and boxes of all your hard-won research is that one day, in the absence of anyone with similar enthusiasm, they may be consigned to the recycling skip.

The scope of this book

This book will focus on the autobiography written chronologically in book form. As this is the most exhaustive work, you can pick and choose what subsets you require. If you feel that the years up until the time you started work were largely unimportant (assuming I cannot convince you otherwise!), then begin your story there. Even if you do this, a few early details may be helpful. The reader likes to have some background, for example:

- when and where you were born
- the names of your parents
- your father's work
- how many siblings you had and your place in the pecking order
- the type of house and area in which you lived
- your education
  etc.

This can be most revealing at a later date if patterns emerge ... even if you have not been able to recognise them yourself.

Considering external assistance

Writing your life story is a large undertaking and some external help and advice might be useful. Hopefully, having read this book you will feel equipped for most eventualities and will even be setting your own milestones. However, sharing these targets and having someone act as a sounding board might be beneficial, particularly if you come to a difficult part in the story.

You will find that chatting about your childhood with someone else, preferably someone who knows little of your life and can therefore make no assumptions, leads to a whole host of ideas pouring forth. One idea triggers another, and before you know it you will have recalled memories you thought were long since gone.

Even if you have decided on a joint book with your partner, it does not necessarily follow that he or she will be the best person to offer objective advice, particularly if you never stop talking about the project!

Finding a writing partner

Various opportunities are open to you:

- a family member ... maybe a sibling or an in-law
- a trusted friend
- a recommendation from a local writers' group
- enrolment in a life writing class – many local authorities offer them
- enrolment on an adult education/university course
- assistance from a professional writing partner.

Some useful contacts can be found at the back of this book.

Setting up a life writing class

If a class is not offered by your local authority, you might like to set up your own. Two or three friends, a local advert and word of mouth will soon establish a small group. A couple of hours a week is all that is required ... and it's great fun.

The local U3A group (University of the Third Age) may offer such a class. If not, they may well be interested in helping you set up such a group under their guidance. (See Useful Addresses at the back of the book.)

Q: I would love my dad to write his life story, but he doesn't like writing.

A: If you father wants to record his life story, there is no reason why he should not do so. Writing is often much easier than people appreciate, and hopefully the many suggestions in this book will help him get started – you might even suggest that you can type up anything he writes, and set him a realistic target: if he can send you few pages about his time doing National Service by the end of the month then you will type it up. Once he's started, it should be plain sailing.

If he finds the process of writing difficult, he may be persuaded to record some of his memories onto tape – again, with your encouragement in the early stages. You could always ask some direct questions to get things started, like, 'Where did you meet Mum?' If he cannot be persuaded to open up in this way, perhaps a friend might have greater success asking the questions – or even a stranger ... it's amazing how people are more inclined to open up to someone when there is no 'history'.

Of course, your father might be citing his inability to write because he doesn't want to relive the past and undertake such a project, which has to be his prerogative, however much you might think otherwise.

Selecting your writing style

Writing in the first person
Most life stories are written in the first person. Initially, you might find it difficult using the word 'I' so much, but it is hard to avoid and you will soon start to feel comfortable with this style. A well-written life story will sound like the author is speaking, and in speech the word 'I' is totally acceptable.

A book written in the third person sounds stilted and uncomfortable. Unless you have very strong reasons for adopting this practice, it is not recommended.

Case study – Alf's milestone

By any stretch of the imagination, Alf had not had an easy life. He had been in care for most of his childhood, and being of a vulnerable disposition did not help his confidence. Alf always managed to steer clear of any trouble, but he had been a victim throughout his life, resulting in his living rough for many years.

Case study – Alf's milestone cont.

Alf's life blossomed when he met Kate and together they found happiness. Alf was encouraged to seek counselling, during which it was suggested that he consider writing his life story, not to be read by anyone, but just to lay certain ghosts to rest. Alf did not have the confidence to write the word 'I', preferring to write in the third person and use 'Alf' throughout. During the project, Alf felt strong enough to show his writing to close friends, resulting in the production of a private book. The party thrown to celebrate the 'book launch' in his care home was one of the proudest moments of Alf's life.

Knowing your audience

Your style will largely be dictated by your audience. You might choose to adopt a chatty style, or perhaps prefer to be more formal if the book is intended for a wider audience, for example former work colleagues.

Feeling comfortable

In most cases you will slip into a certain style without thinking about it, just as if you were writing a letter. It is important that you feel comfortable with how you write and do not over-analyse it. Just be yourself.

It is difficult to contrive a style. For example, if you are not noted for your humour, it is unlikely that your book will be a laugh a minute, but that won't make it any less enjoyable for the reader. If you try to act out of character and be someone you are not the book might be a disappointment to those who know and love you.

Being yourself

Interestingly, men and women tend to write different sorts of books. As a rule, women are very open and are far more comfortable about including everything in their book, 'warts and all'. Men have a tendency to be more conservative, being less inclined to share thoughts and feelings. This is probably a reflection of society; men are not encouraged to share at such an intimate level – women do it with their female friends all the time.

While these are observations gleaned from working with scores of people at an intimate level, they are a generalisation; individuals will fall into the different categories.

Ultimately, there is no right or wrong way. The choice is yours … this is your book.

Choosing a title

There is no need to finalise the title for a long while yet, but you might want to choose a provisional title for your book so that the project seems all the more real. If you haven't given your title any thought, you might like to consider something intriguing to catch attention, rather than 'The Life Story of Joe Soap' or 'I did it my way'.

Drawing upon a theme from your life is a good starting point, perhaps a reference to your career. For example, 'Tending to Care' was written by a nurse, while 'A Balance Sheet of Life' was the work of an accountant.

Other ideas are:

- A quotation – Unto the Breach Dear Friends
- Something intriguing – No Pie on Payday
- A family saying – Catch Yourself on Mrs
- A verse from the Bible – They Shall Inherit the Earth
- A song title – Don't Forget to Remember
- A favourite hymn – The Wings of a Dove

You can have great fun with this, but don't worry if nothing immediately springs to mind; something is likely to come to you during the writing of the book.

Case study – Vera's dream

Sometimes Len and I would go to bed early and read for a while – Marsha would be in her own room, also reading. With the paper-thin walls of the prefab, you could always hear what anyone said. I'd sometimes do the weekly accounts in bed, placing the book on my knees and drawing my feet up – this would also help to keep me warm as the prefab was never that cosy once the fire had died down. Each time I drew my knees up, it caused a draught in the bed. Len, feeling cold, would push my knees down flat, saying, 'No Albert Halls,' referring to my upright knees. We'd argue good-naturedly, and Marsha would pipe up, 'You two fighting again over Albert Halls?' As this happened so often, I said, 'If ever I write a book, I'll call it "No Albert Halls".'

No Albert Halls was published in 2005.

Checklist

- Who is going to read your book?
- What type of record are you looking to produce?
- Are you writing on your own or is it a joint book?
- Do you require any external assistance?

Assignments

- If you already have a title in mind, write it down – it will make the project more of a reality.

❧   Write the introduction to your book explaining why you are writing, who it is for and what you intend to include. This will be revised later, but the exercise will help you to focus on what you want; it will also help you to feel comfortable with your writing style.

Getting Organised

3

By now you should know:

- that you want to write
- who the book is for
- whether this is to be a solo or joint project
- the type of project you require.

However, before your enthusiasm carries you away, it is important to get organised.

Choosing your writing medium

Writing in longhand

Using a pen and paper is the easiest, most versatile and potentially most creative way to write. You can write where you want and when you want – in the garden, on your lap whilst watching snooker on TV, or even at three o'clock in the morning in bed ... assuming you have a tolerant partner!

Millions of books have been written in longhand and, whatever anyone says about modern technology, this will undoubtedly be the formula for millions more.

The most important thing is to complete the manuscript. Once written, it is easy to get it typed. There is nothing wrong with a photocopied handwritten manuscript in a ring binder, but with so many options available you will probably prefer a presentation that is easier on the eye.

Plenty of suggestions for presentation are provided in Chapter 13. If you are intending to leave the manuscript in a handwritten format, it is certainly worth reading that chapter first ... unless you want to rewrite it all.

Q: My handwriting is terrible – will I have to write it out again before I send it to a typist?

A: The general rule of thumb is that if you can read it, so can a typist. They are used to all sorts of scrawl and certainly do not expect a work of art.

If there are some particularly bad bits, like the anecdote you wrote in bed after a dinner party with friends, then you might want to rewrite it, but otherwise it should be all right. If you use a shorthand, like writing 'E' for your friend Elizabeth and 'NCL' for Newcastle, you will need to provide a key. Writing names and places in block capitals is also helpful.

Tapping on a typewriter

If your typewriter is your trusted friend, then by all means use it. It may be slightly less flexible than pen and paper, but if sitting at your typewriter is where you feel at your most creative, then this is the tool for you.

Bear in mind that certain forms of presentation may require your manuscript to be word processed at a later stage. Again, please refer to Chapter 13.

Using a word processor

Many people love their word processor and wonder how they ever managed without it. They feel inspired, creative, liberated. If this is you, then your choice has already been made.

Word processors can be a dedicated machine or a word processing program on a computer. In either case it is worth ensuring that yours is compatible with modern systems, or at least that there is an upgrade path. It is sometimes difficult making disks from older systems work with modern printers, which could cause headaches when it comes to printing your book. Some investigation early on could save much anguish later.

Any new personal computer or laptop will be ideal. See Chapter 14 on Production for further information.

If you are familiar with an older word processor, you will be pleasantly surprised how easy the newer systems are to use, but it still might be worth a few lessons. Most adult education colleges offer word processing courses for total beginners. These are often subsidised or even free. Your local library or adult education college will be happy to offer advice.

Case study – Asif gives up in frustration

Asif was full of enthusiasm as he began to write the story of his life, a project he had been considering for years. He had made a solid start when a friend suggested he buy a word processor. Asif, forever one to do things properly, immediately went along to his local computer shop to investigate things further. He met a very enthusiastic young man and before he knew it, Asif came away with an all-singing all-dancing wonder machine. It was a bit more than he had intended to pay, but he was assured that it would do everything he ever wanted.

> ## Case study – Asif gives up in frustration cont.
>
> For the next five months Asif persevered with his new toy, but however much he read the manual, he just felt that he was going backwards. Jasbinder tried to encourage him by suggesting that he go to a class at the local college, but Asif would not be defeated.
>
> The wonder machine now sits in the spare room gathering dust ... along with the first two and a half chapters of Asif's manuscript.

Knowing your limits

If you are unfamiliar with word processors, please consider carefully before deciding to write your life story with one. For every person who is a fanatical convert to computers there are those who shudder at the very thought of using them.

If you want to learn to use a word processor, a good time is when it comes to reviewing and editing your manuscript. At least if you do give up, the all-important information has already been captured.

Recording onto tape

For those for whom writing is difficult, or if you feel particularly comfortable with tape recorders, this could be the perfect medium for you. It also has the added benefit of retaining a record of your voice for posterity, something that will delight future generations in years to come.

Dictating your life story requires discipline in terms of preparing notes beforehand. It is also wise to keep a list of the subjects covered on each tape and in which order – if only to know where to add a stray anecdote if the tapes are transcribed. The tapes should be given reference numbers, and annotated to show the years covered and the date the recording was made.

Video and DVD options

Those who feel comfortable about a visual record might like to produce a DVD or video in the privacy of their own home. Commercial companies can be found to undertake such services at a price, although, for the non-technically minded, most requirements can usually be met by someone in the family or a helpful friend.

Making the decision

You may well choose a combination of the above, but whatever technology you employ, it is worth keeping a pen and notepad handy for when inspiration strikes.

Ultimately you should choose the medium with which you feel the most comfortable and creative.

Finding your own special place

Getting comfortable

People differ as to where they like to work; some rove around as the whim takes them, others prefer always to be in the same place. However, even for the itinerant, it is worth having a base – your own special place to keep your manuscript, notes and any memorabilia you collect.

Writing is going to occupy much of your time over the coming months, so if you can set a room aside, so much the better. This will also allow you to leave notes and pictures spread out to inspire you when it comes to your next session.

Remaining undisturbed

Find a place where you can reminisce and let your mind wander undisturbed. It is worth making this area personal to you, a place where you want to work – a comfy chair, good lighting, perhaps the odd picture or two and plenty of writing materials so that you don't have to run off and find another pen just as the words are starting to flow.

Q: I don't want to tell anyone that I'm writing a book until it is finished. Is this possible?

A: It might be hard to keep your writing a secret from anyone with whom you share a house, but others should present few problems. Some cunning may be required if information or pictures are required from those sources not in the know, but this should not be difficult ... after all, they have no idea that you are writing a book.

Not telling too many people about it also avoids you being asked, 'How's the book coming along?' After several months this can become quite tiresome. A secret book also provides a wonderful excuse for a surprise 'launch'.

Getting organised

Setting up a simple filing system

Once you start reminiscing you will be amazed how the floodgates open. It is important that these precious pieces of information are not lost. A simple filing system can save a lot of grief later ... especially if it means you don't lose any treasured photos you may have borrowed.

As it is worth collating the information in chapters, a concertina file might come in useful. However, a number of large envelopes or some box files will do just as well. One author even collected cardboard tomato boxes from the local supermarket. The protruding corners made for easy stacking – they were ideal ... all 21 of them!

Having the right tools for the job

Once you have decided to write your life story, it is worth keeping several notepads around the house, especially on the bedside table. You can guarantee that just as you are about to nod off to sleep some fascinating detail will filter into your mind ... the subconscious is amazing like that. You then either spend a sleepless night trying to ensure you don't forget it, or you torture yourself in the morning trying to remember what was so earth shattering. Write it down.

It is also worth keeping some paper and a pen on you at all times, just in case a random comment at the bus stop sparks off another flash of inspiration. A notepad and pen in the car is also a useful idea.

Spoiling yourself
Some people like to buy a special pen and a good quality notebook, the latter acting as a master reference for all the notepads around the house and for any inspirational ideas. A hardback book in which to write the actual manuscript is not advisable – a lever-arch file and loose-leaf sheets allow greater flexibility in adding information at a later stage.

Being prepared
Office superstores provide great value and are well worth a visit to stock up on useful items for the project. These might include:

- notepads
- lined A4 pads (preferably with margins and pre-punched holes)
- pens
- pencils
- rubber
- treasury tags
- paper clips
- coloured highlighter pens
- lever-arch file
- concertina file for pictures and documents (box file and envelopes will suffice)
- dividers
- hole punch.

If you are using a word processor and printer ensure you have back-up disks and a spare cartridge, for a typewriter a spare ribbon, and for both plenty of paper.

Establishing a back-up system

Even if you are writing the manuscript in longhand or using a typewriter it is worth thinking about taking a photocopy. This is particularly important if you send a chapter or two to a friend to proofread, or perhaps to your brother to check a few facts about your early life. However, even a wayward cup of coffee, a hungry dog or an over-exuberant grandchild can soon put paid to many hours of work.

Backing-up your word processor

If your writing is on computer, back-ups become all the more essential. Modern systems can back up at pre-specified intervals, for example every ten minutes, without any interference to the user. This is worthwhile in case you inadvertently forget to save the file or there is a system crash. Having to retype hours of work is frustrating to say the least.

A back-up of the files used every session is good practice. It may even be worth keeping a spare back-up disk/CD with a neighbour and swapping it every week or two for further peace of mind, or sending the file via email to a friend.

Setting provisional targets

Recognising how you work

You may be the sort of person who likes to set time aside regularly or you might attack the project in bursts and then leave it for several weeks before recommencing. Summer is a busy time for some and so they undertake the bulk of the writing between autumn and early spring. Then there are the 'morning people', whilst others prefer to burn the midnight oil. Work to your strengths.

Booking time to write

Some people find booking time in their diary a useful discipline as events can easily eat into the time earmarked for writing. An 'appointment' in the diary can make time spent writing more official.

Finding time to write in the early stages when there is enthusiasm by the bucketful will not be a problem, but once deep into the project it can be a different matter. Most writers recognise that some discipline is important to overcome the difficult times.

This project is meant to be enjoyable, not a chore, so be realistic in your planning. It does not matter if your manuscript takes longer to complete than anticipated ... as long as it gets completed. Recognise your strengths and weaknesses and plan accordingly.

Allowing thinking time

You are likely to be thinking about this project for a great many of your waking hours, especially early on ... sometimes to the frustration of those around you! Mulling things over in your mind is a vital part of the process and so if you don't write much in some of the sessions you have set aside, don't worry about it. Just because you are not writing, does not mean you are not working.

Having a launch date in mind

Although it is hard to estimate how long the project will take, some people like to have a timescale in mind; a provisional target for the launch of the book can help focus the mind.

Q: How long will it take me to write?

A: Once inspired, some people sit down and write reams, completing a comprehensive record in as little as three or four months. For others the research alone can take much longer and they work on their book for years.

For those setting aside one or two sessions a week, a year is a realistic target in which to write and edit a manuscript. Depending on the type of presentation you require, especially if pictures are to be included, a further few months could be added to the schedule.

As projects often take much longer than expected, if you are thinking of finishing your book for your 68th birthday, it might also be worth considering your Ruby Wedding Anniversary eight months later as a fall-back date.

Establishing bite-sized chunks

If you decide to work towards a target date you can break the project down into manageable sections. This will be much easier to do after the brainstorming in Chapter 4 when you decide chapter headings.

Checklist

- Do you feel comfortable with the writing medium you have chosen? You don't want to get deflected in your resolve to write ... you will encounter enough distractions without adding one more.
- Have you collated the various materials you are going to need, and organised a place to keep these and all the memorabilia which will soon be descending upon you?
- If you have a deadline for the book, is it realistic?

Assignments

- Decide what targets are most likely to motivate you and help you in this project – maybe a certain number of hours or pages of writing a week. If the discipline helps, allocate some time in your diary for writing.
- Read a few autobiographies, not necessarily of famous people. This will give you some idea of the sort of book you might like. Interestingly, badly written books can teach you more as they show you what to avoid.

Planning the Structure

4

Planning the framework for your book and establishing chapter headings is surprisingly easy and enjoyable. A well spent hour or two here will provide an excellent provisional structure.

Please don't expect everything to be perfect first time. The structure will be continually revised throughout the course of the project, and can even be reviewed again once the manuscript has been written.

For ease of analysis, the structure here is written from the viewpoint of a single life story followed chronologically. Ideas for alternative structures, joint books and family histories are discussed in the next chapter.

Defining the parameters of the book

Deciding where to start

When you were considering the sort of record you wanted, you may have had an idea of where the book should begin. Techniques like flashbacks and turning points are covered in Chapter 7, but unless you have strong views to the contrary, describing what you know of your ancestors is always a good place to start.

You may feel that you know relatively little about your family background, but what you do know is likely to be of great interest to future generations. The countries from where the family originated or lived for many years, the industries in which they worked, the size of the families, social class and religion can all help to set the scene, particularly as families now tend to be smaller and more mobile.

There is no need to embark on any in-depth research just yet, although if a great uncle is still around it would certainly be worth finding out what he knows. It is invariably the case that most people know far more about their families than they appreciate or consider important.

The other popular place to start is with the birth of the author ... 'I was born at home in the small hours of the morn-ing on ...' Of course, even with this it is possible to reflect back on the sort of family into which you were born.

Deciding where to finish

Most people like to bring their writing up to the present day, but you may have another milestone in mind, for example the millennium, your 50th wedding anniversary, the birth of your last grandchild, or your 75th birthday at the end of next year. Greater attention will be given to endings in Chapter 11.

The proposed end point of the book may well alter during the writing of your manuscript. With this in mind it is usually worth bringing your story up to the present when thinking about your chapter headings.

Q: How long should the book be?

A: There are no hard and fast rules – stop writing whenever you feel that you've said enough. However, it is worth being aware of false modesty – for the time being, simply write anything and everything.

A typical book will usually be between 40,000 and 80,000 words, about 150–300 pages. However, don't feel daunted. This only equates to 15–30 pages per chapter, and once you get going you will be amazed at how much you write.

If you are intending to have the book bound, you should be aiming for at least 150 sides, although the inclusion of pictures and a few introductory pages will account for some of these.

Identifying chapter headings

Once you have established where you want the book to start and finish you are ready to jot down some chapter headings for your initial book structure. These are purely to help you categorise broad areas of your life, and might be as shown in Figure 1.

> Family background
> Childhood and schooldays
> The war years
> My first job
> National Service
> Back to work
> Marriage
> Early married life
> Changing career
> The family grows
> Retirement
> Grandchildren
> Voluntary work

Figure 1 Initial book structure

Typically there might be 10 or 15 categories that, by and large, cover the main areas of your life. As these categories should be obvious, there is no reason why this phase of the process should take more than ten minutes – half an hour at the outside. If you have a CV, even a very old one, it could be very helpful here.

The book *Times of Our Lives* follows a typical life of someone born before or during the Second World War. For those to whom this applies, reference to the book should prove beneficial. Details can be found under Further Reading.

Breaking down the chapters

Obviously huge areas have been ignored and others do not fit comfortably under any heading, for example, friends, holidays, hobbies and pets, all of which may overlap several chapters.

Even at this stage you will probably be able to subdivide some headings, like 'Childhood', for example, if you moved several times, were evacuated or perhaps lived overseas.

A large category such as 'Family Life' covering a span of 30 years or more, might be better divided into two chapters entitled 'Early Married Life' and 'The Family Grows'. Of course, references to the children are also likely to appear in other chapters as well, although how much you include about them will be covered in greater length in Chapter 11. A long and diverse working life may well also require several chapters.

Q: How many years should a typical chapter cover?

A: This depends on how interesting the period is that you are considering. For example, if you were evacuated, even though this might have been for only 18 months, a separate chapter would be appropriate. There will be so much to relate, not least how you adjusted to the upheaval, and a description of your new and strange environment. In later life when there tend to be more set routines, a chapter can cover twenty years or more.

You will normally have a feel for significant areas in your life which justify a chapter in their own right. If an imbalance exists it is likely to be ironed out as you are writing – you will feel that you have come to a natural chapter break. Other concerns can be addressed when the book is reviewed for balance at the end.

Brainstorming

This is where the creative process begins as you mentally trawl through your life and let the ideas flow.

Write each of your chapter headings on a separate sheet of paper. Then, concentrating on one of the headings, write down whatever topics come to mind. They don't have to be in any order.

For some headings there might only be three or four topics listed; for others there may be dozens. For the latter category, rewrite the list grouping common areas together, possibly under a general heading. This might look something like Figure 2.

Keeping focused

During this brainstorming you will undoubtedly be bombarded with detailed memories. It helps if you can capture the essence of your thoughts in just a few words because we think 12 times faster than we write!

What you are really looking for here are broad topics, but it is important that no precious recollections are lost. If specific memories flit into your mind, jot them down and then move on, concentrating on the more general areas. There will be an opportunity for more detailed brainstorming before you start writing the manuscript.

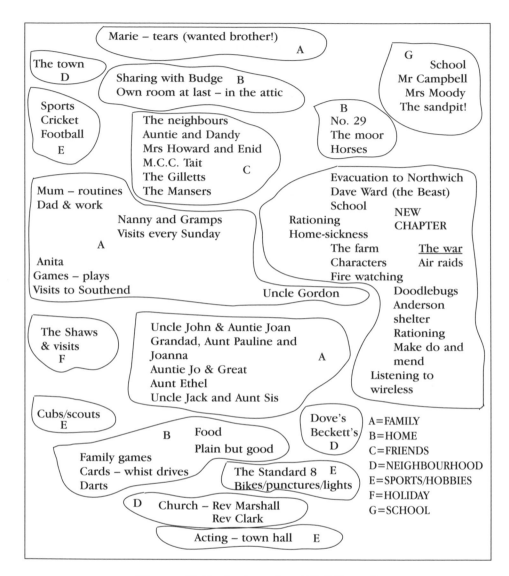

Figure 2 Brainstorming 'Childhood'

Revising the initial book structure

These topics from Figure 2 can now be incorporated into the
initial book structure (Figure 1) to produce Figure 3.

   – Family background
       Parents in service at Cliveden
       Mum's family
       Dad's family
       Their childhoods and how they met

   – Childhood + school days
       Family
       Home
       Friends
       Neighbourhood
       School
       Sports/hobbies
       Holidays

   – Evacuation
       Dad departing
       Air raids
       Changes encountered
       Rationing
       School + friends
       Countryside

   – Return to London
       Devastation
       Home (new)
       School
       Scouts

Figure 3 Section of revised book structure

In the above example the chapter dealing with the war has been divided into two chapters entitled 'Evacuation' and 'Return to London'.

We are aiming at balance throughout the book, but this won't necessarily emerge immediately because at this stage we cannot tell how long each section will be. However, beware of 17 chapters about work and only one on the family ... and that one including golf and holidays!

Remaining organised
You may find that you have made many more notes than those transcribed onto the revised book structure. It is

important that these are not lost. Place these sheets of paper in your filing system for future reference – you haven't finished with the book structure yet!

Introducing a time line

Against this revised book structure you can add a time line to map dates to the framework. This helps to organise facts and reduce the risk of omitting significant areas.

Some dates will spring readily to mind:

- birth
- years at school
- starting work
- marriage
  etc.

Other dates may need a little more thought:

- births of three younger brothers
- visiting Bob in Canada
- meeting your partner
- buying first car
- Jim dying
- being promoted to section leader
  etc.

It is not essential that all dates be precise, the general period is enough ... although with something like your wedding day someone else may appreciate you getting it right!

Adding key historical dates

You can also include key dates of history which come into your story and which help you place where you were. We are only looking at major events here, those that come readily to mind and dates that trip off the tongue. A more detailed analysis comes later.

Such events might include:

- 1939 – war started (September)
- 1945 – war ended (May Europe – August Japan)
- 1947 – severe winter freeze
- 1948 – NHS founded (Betty training as nurse)
- 1952 – King George VI dies
- 1953 – Coronation (got our first TV set)
- 1956 – Clean Air Act (living in London – smog!)
  etc.

Case study – Slapdash Terry

Terry had always been someone who got stuck right in when it came to starting a new project: 'Strike while the iron's hot' was his motto. Eileen wished he paid more attention to preparation – perhaps the kitchen units might shut properly if he did!

When it came to writing his life story, Terry was right in there as usual – despite Eileen's suggestion that a few notes in advance might not be a bad idea. He may only have been a literary Lilliputian, but the first four or five chapters simply fell out of Terry's pen. Eileen was a little concerned on several occasions when she wondered aloud if Terry had mentioned a particular episode, only to see him scurrying to his den. But, by and large, the manuscript was progressing well.

The real problem came when Terry had to lay his writing aside for three months. He had not lost enthusiasm, it was just that the grandchildren stayed for three weeks, then there was his knee replacement operation followed by a holiday ...

Terry did eventually finish his writing. However, by now he was bored with the project and couldn't be bothered to review it. He had it bound, and in fact it was not a bad effort, but Eileen knew that it was somewhat higgledy-piggledy and could have been so much better ... and she had to bite her tongue when she noticed that he'd forgotten to mention his brother George.

Weaving it all together

Figure 4 shows part of the fully revised book structure, including the time line.

	Year	My age
– Family background	pre 1930	
Parents in service at Cliveden		
Mum's family		
Dad's family		
Their childhoods and how they met		
– Childhood + school days	1930–9	0–9
Family		
Home		
Friends		
Neighbourhood		
School		
Sports/hobbies		
Holidays		
– Evacuation	1939–42	9–12
Dad departing		
Air raids	1940	
Changes encountered		
Rationing	1940–54	
School + friends		
Countryside		
– Return to London	1942–5	12–15
Devastation		
Home (new)		
School		
Scouts		
Doodlebugs	1944	
VE Day	1945 (May 8th)	

Figure 4 Integrated structure with time line and historical dates

Some subject areas fit neatly in one chapter while others span several. Ideas for dealing with overlapping subjects are considered in the next chapter.

Taking a break

You can feel satisfied that on a few sheets of paper you have the essence of your book ... now all you have to do is break down each chapter into much more detail and then write the manuscript! However, all that can come later. Your head is probably spinning too much to consider doing anything more just yet. Relax – you've earned it.

Checklist

- Are you happy with your start and end points?
- Are you confident that your book structure covers all the major episodes you want to include?
- Think about friends and family who might potentially read the book. Have you included something about each of them?

Assignments

- Look at other autobiographies and see how the books are structured and what material is included.
- Consider asking someone who knows you well to review the intended structure of your book.
- Flick through *Times of Our Lives* to assist with your thoughts on the structure of your book.

Considering Alternative Structures

5

This chapter provides ideas for different book structures and how to accommodate other contributions.

Thinking laterally

You can be creative in how you structure your book. A few of the more conventional ideas are listed here, but feel free to let your mind wander.

Expressing your life in time spans

The early years of our life can usually be associated with certain ages. The following would be an example:

  0–5 Pre-school and family background
  5–11 Primary and junior schools
11–16 Secondary school
16–18 Early working life

18–21   National Service
21–25   Meeting Mary and settling down
25–30   Early married life and children.

If this pattern can be followed relatively neatly throughout the later stages of your life as well, you might like to consider structuring your writing in this way.

Using the decades

A variation on the above theme is to write your book in decades. These can either be the decades of your life or of the twentieth century:

My life	*The twentieth century*
Early years	1930s
My teens	1940s
My twenties	1950s
My thirties	1960s
etc.	etc.

Placing your life in specific compartments

The methods expressed so far have been consistent with a chronological approach to writing your life story. If you want something a little more adventurous you could consider writing in various compartments each spanning the whole of your life:

Jim the student
Jim the family man
Jim the working man
Jim the friend
Jim the sportsman
Jim the traveller
Jim the poet

Unless there are several quite distinct areas of your life, this is probably not a recommended structure. However, these ideas might help you to think more laterally about your own project.

Mixing structures

Of course, even within the more conventional chronological book structure, there is nothing to stop you introducing creative chapters. You might want to write about 'The Swinging Sixties', 'Life in my Thirties' or 'My Thespian Career'. Alternatively, you can include a 'Soapbox' where you put the world to rights, or perhaps have a more reflective, 'What If ...' chapter.

Undertaking a joint project

There is no limit on the options available to you or the number of contributors to a book. For example, seven brothers and sisters can each write a chapter for a family archive. Cousins, business partners or friends joining forces provide other options.

Such projects tend to have a simple structure with each contributor writing either a chapter or section of the book.

There is greater scope for interweaving chapters when the book is written by a married couple, or by different generations of a family.

Writing as a couple

This is a very popular project for those who enjoy working closely together. Having a sounding board and someone else who can share the joys and frustrations of writing is a great benefit. Additionally, such a book tends to be more well-rounded, capturing the personalities of both parties.

There are two main types of project you might like to consider here:

- equal partnership
- one partner taking the lead.

Contributing as equal partners

Each partner will write about their background, childhood and early life before they met. Once their lives join together, the subsequent chapters will be written by either party. Some subjects like children and work will probably fall quite neatly into place, but decisions will have to be made as to who writes about holidays, grandchildren, etc.

Of course, there is no reason why certain subjects should not be written about by both partners. Indeed, for events like when you first met it can be fascinating to read accounts from two different view-points.

Q: My husband and I are working on a joint book. How much should we confer about our writing?

A: For subjects that clearly have to be written by one partner, like early childhood, it may help to discuss ideas to stimulate the memory. Where you are writing about the same subject, for example your wedding day, it is better to write independently as the interest often lies in the difference of recollections and emphasis. However, this can lead to some disappointment ... for example, the man who described the highlight of his wedding day as seeing a peregrine falcon on the way to the church!

Weaving the book together

The two most popular ways of interspersing chapters can be seen in Figures 5 and 6.

As can be seen, whichever structure is chosen, once the two lives come together the rest of the book follows the same format.

Of course, as with the sole author, the structure can be refined as you proceed; the only difference is that it involves a little communication.

If both partners choose to write their independent life stories there is no reason why the two accounts should not be placed after each other and bound in the same cover.

However, this is not so much a joint autobiography, as two separate autobiographies produced in the same volume.

Bill – Meet the ancestors
Dot – In the beginning ...
Bill – Childhood
Dot – Life in India
Dot – Coming to England
Bill – Schooldays
Dot – Schooling in Malvern
Dot – Back to India
Bill – Apprenticeship
Bill – National Service
Dot – Training as a nurse
Bill – Holt Industries
Dot – Qualified
Bill – The cycling club
Bill – Meeting Dorothy
Dot – Bill

The two lives coming together

Dot – Early married life
Bill – Going solo
Bill – Forming ACA
Dot – The family grows
Bill – Selling up
Bill – Moving to the Lake District
Dot – Round the world
Dot – Grandchildren
Bill – What next?

Figure 5 Contributing to chapters – method 1

One partner taking the lead
While many couples are equally enthusiastic about the prospect of writing, more often than not the passion for the project is weighted heavily in favour of one of the parties. George might be writing his book, but Irene is happy to contribute a chapter about her early life for the benefit of the grandchildren.

In such a case, it is recommended that George structures the book as if he were doing it entirely by himself.

Bill – Meet the ancestors
Childhood
Schooldays
Apprenticeship
National Service
Holt Industries
The cycling club
Meeting Dorothy
Dot – In the beginning ...
Life in India
Coming to England
Schooling in Malvern
Back to India
Training as a nurse
Qualified!
Bill

The two lives coming

Dot – Early married life
Bill – Going solo
Bill – Forming ACA
Dot – The family grows
Bill – Selling up
Bill – Moving to the Lake District
Dot – Round the world
Dot – Grandchildren
Bill – What next?

Figure 6 Contributing to chapters – method 2

Tying in the partner's contribution

When George gets to the point in his story where he disappears off on honeymoon with Irene he might now write something along the lines of:

'Before I continue with our married life together, Irene has provided a few pages about her family and early life.'

Irene's chapter covering the time until she married George is then inserted, after which George continues with his book.

If Irene is happy to add some further material later, perhaps about the children in their early years, this can similarly be tied in at the appropriate stage in the narrative.

Case study – Ted changes his mind

Ted had always wanted to write about his days in the Royal Navy Voluntary Reserve – the 'wavy navy' as he called it. Beryl was happy to encourage him, not least as he was getting under her feet now that he had finally retired. She suggested that while he was at it, Ted might as well bring his story up to the present day.

Ted immersed himself in his new project and all went smoothly until it came to writing about the family. He had been away for much of the time when the children were growing up and did not know what to write. In a flash of inspiration Ted asked Beryl if she would write a few pages. Beryl was flattered, and wrote a chapter about the children – indeed she also wrote a second chapter about her early life to provide a balanced book for the grandchildren.

Ted was delighted ... he even learned a few things about Beryl and the children in the process! All he had to do was rewrite the introduction to his book to explain the new format.

Writing as separate generations

Asking the children to contribute
A person writing an autobiography might ask the children if they would like to contribute a few pages about their

childhoods. These can then either be included within the body of the book, or alternatively as appendices, whichever is more appropriate. See Chapter 13 for ideas.

There is no reason why other members of the family, particularly siblings or grandchildren, should not be given a similar opportunity.

In this instance, the book is likely to be written by the grandparent with various small contributions from other family members.

Writing as a family

A more adventurous project might be for several family members to contribute to one book. They can decide their own content, or all write on the same subject. A title like 'My Childhood' would provide a fascinating record, especially among the different generations.

It may be that a grandparent acts as narrator for the book, providing the framework and introducing the various family members at the appropriate places.

Such a project needs strong coordination but is a hugely enjoyable and rewarding experience.

Family histories

The options available depend on the complexity of the project. Most people embarking on an extensive study will have a framework in mind. Usually this will collate branches of the family, the length and detail of the branch depending on how much information has been gathered. It is advisable to include a family tree depicting that part of the branch at the front of the section. Where there are many branches over several generations, an overview at the front of the book – a 'roadmap' – is always helpful for the reader.

Where the project covers only a few generations, a popular alternative is to divide the book into sections for each generation. This works particularly well where each generation falls neatly into a broad range of years.

Whatever structure is adopted for the family history, a few lines in the introduction explaining how you decided to tackle the project will be most helpful. This might also include how you dealt with contributions from relatives or other third parties. Usually these will be placed within the main body of the book, although an alternative preference is for them to be collated in a separate appendix with reference being made to this at the appropriate point in the narrative. Again, explaining your thought process in the introduction will aid the reader's enjoyment of the book.

Checklist

- Is there anything else you can add to the structure of your book?
- Is their anyone you might ask to contribute to your book?

Assignment

- Review your book structure to see if it can be improved in the light of this chapter

Preparing to Tell Your Story 6

This chapter considers some writing points that you might like to bear in mind before putting pen to paper.

Don't try to digest everything – read through the chapter and then let ideas wander into your mind over the next few days. Perhaps after you've written a chapter or two you can revisit this chapter for more ideas, and again prior to reading through the entire manuscript before the final edit.

A selection of extracts from various amateur writers can be found in Chapter 8. These might also be of assistance as you consider your own writing style.

Feeling comfortable with yourself

Being yourself
The most important advice in this whole chapter is for you to be yourself. People love us for being us, with all of our little

imperfections and foibles. If in our writing we try to make ourselves out to be someone we are not, it will not ring true.

As this is likely to be a purely private book, those reading it will know you very well. You will remember some events differently from your readers – that is only to be expected. The memory also plays tricks from time to time. However, if the reader perceives that history is being rewritten on too many occasions your book will lose credibility.

Remember, your readers are on your side. Just be yourself.

Striking the right balance

Most people err on the side of modesty rather than arrogance. However, beware, a book dripping with humility can grate with the reader just as much as arrogance.

Case study – Frank's perfect marriage

Frank was a man's man. He lived life to the full and called a spade a spade. His marriage to Mollie had been a bit of a rumbustious affair, but they had muddled through, largely because Mollie knew when to bite her tongue. Frank had a bit of a temper as the neighbours well knew – the fact that he had been a drill sergeant in the army probably accounted for that.

When Mollie died, Frank decided it was time to write his life story. He was quite open and fair in most of what he wrote – he knew he was no saint. Strangely, though, his recollections of his marriage to Mollie differed quite significantly from those of his readers. The words 'idyllic', 'harmonious' and 'never a cross word ...' did not automatically spring to their minds!

Sharing secrets

How much you choose to reveal about yourself is obviously up to you. However, sharing a secret with the reader, even a small one like a hitherto unknown nickname or an embarrassing moment from your childhood, will endear you to your audience.

Many high-profile biographies fall into the trap of keeping the reader at arm's length. Having reached the final page it is all too easy to feel that you know no more about the person than before you started.

Being natural

Writing the way you speak

> ### Case study – Roy lives on
>
> Prior to his death, Roy wrote his life story. In fact he had so enjoyed the experience that he even wrote a sequel. Each volume was quite large, but there again, Roy was never one to use one word where 27 would fit just as well.
>
> In the address at his funeral, a few pages of Roy's first book were read to the congregation. Afterwards several people commented that they could hear Roy speaking through his book. Roy lives on.

As long as you are not trying to be too clever, you will easily fall into a comfortable writing style. The best way to achieve this is to write the way you speak.

The use of a thesaurus can add colour and diversity to your manuscript, but try not to use those words where you have to look up the meaning. If you don't even know what they mean they are clearly not in your everyday vocabulary.

Using humour

If you are humorous by nature, this will reflect in your writing. Anecdotes are the usual form of introducing humour, and a few well-chosen stories will add to your story. However, think carefully about what you write – once in print it's there forever ... and what sounded like a good idea at the time might be a little insensitive.

Additionally, the odd tale against yourself will engage the reader and make it easier to tell a gentle story against someone else.

Being thorough

Not discounting anything

The usual adage about writing a book is that, come the end, the waste-paper basket is full of golden nuggets that failed to make the final cut. However, if they are golden nuggets why shouldn't they be included?

The fascination in a life story is the detail – the fact that a memory has jumped back into your consciousness after 50 or 60 years must mean something. Include it.

Substituting yourself with a grandparent

A useful test here is to substitute yourself with your grandmother or grandfather. If they had written a book, what would you want to know? The answer has surely got to be, 'Everything', or, at the very least, 'Whatever they chose to say.'

If your grandmother had confided the fact that her favourite colour was sky-blue and that as a child she had an imaginary friend called Boris, you'd be delighted. It might also explain your vivid imagination or why your favourite colour is sky-blue.

Leaving the editing for later

Just because you write something early on does not mean that it has to appear in the final book if, upon review, you feel that the narrative has become tedious. However, it is easier to make such decisions when you consider the balance of the entire manuscript rather than a few pages at a time.

Obviously, boring your reader is something to be avoided, but care has to be exercised to ensure that it is not simply modesty speaking. Again, ask the question, 'What would you have wanted your grandfather to have eliminated from his writing?' At this stage, keep it in. Your readers can always skip pages if they wish – the odds are that they won't.

Editing will be discussed at greater length in Chapter 12 when it comes to reviewing your manuscript.

Assuming nothing

Whoever your intended audience, it is best to assume no knowledge by the reader. While your children are well aware of the fact that Grandpa had a wooden leg, what about the as yet unborn great-grandchild? Without the relevant knowledge, the story of Grandpa sawing off his leg when he trapped it in a cattle grid takes on a different meaning!

Providing a reference point

Increasingly fewer people know what ten bob was – how many less in 30 years' time? However, the fact that it is 50p is of less interest than providing a reference as to what that could buy. Your Dad was earning £3.15s.0d a week at the time ... and he was manager of the local cinema in charge of 12 staff.

For those who wish to include imperial and decimal values, a conversion chart can be found at the back of the book.

Similarly, everyone knows that Gordon was your best mate, but mentioning that you met on a works outing to the Isle of Wight adds a bit of background to someone who virtually became one of the family. If Gordon suddenly appears in the story from nowhere it might confuse some potential future readers.

Of course, not everything can be explained, and if Vera Lynn is not known in 50 years' time at least it might make the reader look up her name in a history book.

Ensuring historical consistency

Thinking as you did at the time

The benefit of hindsight can alter how we tell a story. Neville Chamberlain has been treated harshly by history in proclaiming 'Peace for our time' ... he was not so universally scorned on 30 September 1938.

The press has made us very familiar with the present royal family, but what were the feelings of the nation on 12 December 1936 when Edward VIII abdicated?

Trying to project your thinking back in time is not easy, but it makes for a great read.

Using the right words

A follow-on from the above point is trying to be as historically accurate as possible. This involves using the right words in the relevant periods of your life.

The list below will evoke different memories:

- wireless set (cat's whisker)
- radiogram
- radio
- record player
- stereo system
- hi-fi
- box brownie
- cine camera.

If you were lucky enough to get a television set for the coronation in 1953 you probably did not call it 'telly', 'TV' or 'the box'. And when did an aeroplane become an airplane or plane?

Taking care with time sequence

It is inevitable that your book will date ... indeed, it is likely to have dated since you first put pen to paper. If you write about your grandchildren, you will probably record their ages and maybe include their pictures. This is fine and is to be expected even though they might be a year older before the book makes its long-awaited appearance.

Where you can be careful is in the use of unspecific timescales. Words and phrases like 'ago' and 'last summer' will be ambiguous unless you link them to when you are writing or provide a date. To write, 'We visited Ralph in Spain two years ago' will be needlessly confusing. The reader will have to refer to the date when the book was written to work out when you mean. It is simpler for the reader if you write, 'We visited Ralph in Spain in 2004,' or, 'We visited Ralph in Spain two years ago, in 2004.'

Telling the story

Setting the context

All good stories need context. Take for example your first school:

- What was it called?
- Where was it?
- What was its size:
  - number of classes?
  - number of teachers?
  - the age range per class?
  - how many children per class?
- Is it still a school – or has it perhaps been converted to a two-bedroomed house (that really shows its size)?

- How far away was it?
- How did you get there?
- Who took you to school?
- Who was the headmaster?
- Who was your teacher?
- What did he/she look like?
- How strict was he/she?
- Who was your best friend?
- Did you stay in touch?
- What forms of punishment were used?
- Were you ever on the receiving end?
- Why?
- If not, why not?
  etc.

All of these facts and hundreds more will be woven into the narrative to create the overall picture.

Utilising the why and the how

Many of the broad facts about our life will be similar to countless thousands of others. What differentiates us is how we interpret those facts – how we did what we did and our intentions behind those actions.

The fact that you went swimming every day of the summer holidays of 1936 is impressive, but what is more interesting is the inspiration behind it: the fact that you had seen Johnny Weissmuller as Tarzan earlier that year and you wanted to be able to swim like him. In fact, you also got into bodybuilding in a small way and started to watch what you ate. What was not so clever, though, was breaking your arm when you fell out of the tree trying to swing on the ivy ... how was a 12-year-old to know that it wouldn't take such weight!

We can also apply these principles to others. Why did your parents live where they did and how did that come about? Think about their circumstances – you may arrive at some interesting conclusions.

Showing not telling

A significant tool used by the storyteller is to impart information by showing rather than telling. Describing the story of Dad hiding Granny's teeth is amusing, but it also shows us that he had a sense of humour and was a real tease. This is far better than writing, 'Dad had a great sense of humour.'

Case study – Jean's Gran

In remembering her grandmother, Jean initially wrote: 'Gran was great, and despite appearances to the contrary, she had a wicked sense of humour.' Asked for an anecdote to illustrate the point, her face lit up. What finally appeared in her book was:

'Gran could come across as severe to those who didn't know her, but nothing could be further from the truth. Despite her widow's weeds, and always sitting bolt upright on a high-backed chair, she was as mischievous as they come. One day Jim and I were playing in the kitchen when we heard the gate squeak – it was the district nurse come to give us the dreaded cod liver oil to keep us "regular". Without blinking, Gran said, "Quick! Under here," as she lifted up her voluminous skirt. Jim and I crawled underneath, clutched her legs and held our breath as we heard the latch lift on the back door. As calm as you like, Gran said, "Sorry, Dot. They're playing outside somewhere. I've no idea where they are. You'd better leave it today." And with that, Dot disappeared. Gran was our hero!'

Including what you don't know

Often what you don't know can be of more interest than what you do, and is certainly worth including. If you don't know the answers say so. The fact that your school was in a poor area is of interest, but it is even more interesting to know that '... while it was in a poor area, we had no concept of rich or poor – we were all the same.'

Similarly, 'I never really thought too much about living through the war; we just carried on as best we could.'

Developing the story

Creating interest from the start

Giving your book a strong opening will engage the reader's attention from the outset.

If you are starting the book at your birth, instead of writing, 'I was born ...' try to think more laterally – perhaps something like this:

> 'I don't know if it was a ploy by my parents to fend off the seven-year itch, but I was born seven years after my elder brother Bob, 14 years into the marriage of my parents, Joe and Joyce Rice.'

As well as imparting a fair bit of information, you have also created some mystique.

Questioning your story

Your story will be obvious to you and you will therefore make many assumptions. Questioning some of these can lead to interesting results.

This is part of the benefit of attending a life writing class, or perhaps having someone to help you. By discussing the writing, it is easier to spot any ambiguities.

Such questioning is of particular importance when writing about growing up abroad or during the war – experiences that may well be far removed from your reader and which therefore need greater explanation.

Case study – Len takes to the air

Len was in meteorology during the war and one of his duties when based in Antigua was to observe weather conditions from the air. In his story he wrote, 'One day, when flying at 2,000 feet, I lost my glasses.'

Len had explained in an earlier chapter that he wore glasses from childhood, so this fact comes as no surprise. What does come as a surprise was that the aeroplane was of First World War issue and had an open cockpit. Without this information, the reason why he lost his glasses and the point of the anecdote is missed.

Embellishing a story

It is important to think through stories to ensure that a good anecdote is not overlooked. A story can often be embellished considerably simply by sifting it over in your mind.

The broad fact may be that you met Mary at a dance. But how did you hear about the dance? You may have seen it advertised in the corner shop when you popped in to buy some sweets because you missed the bus. You missed the bus because you had been chatting to Fred to find out the Test Match score. So, indirectly, the reason you met and later married Mary was because of cricket ... and Mary hates cricket! This is a much better story than the bland fact of meeting Mary at a dance.

It is often when lying in bed that you will be able to develop stories in this way ... but don't forget to have the notepad handy.

Q: How much artistic licence can I use?

A: You are the best judge of this.

Ultimately you don't want your book to be or sound false, but often you will find that the details are already there for a better story with a little thought.

Some people like to use speech in their writing – even when reporting a conversation at which it is obvious they could not have been present. This can be a useful device, but may come across as a little strange, certainly if over-used. If in doubt, leave this for when you write your novel.

Further advice regarding speech appears in the next chapter.

Engaging the reader

Helping the reader to empathise

Nothing warms a reader to the author more than shared emotions. We all feel them, and therefore empathise with the writer.

All emotions can be used, but if you feel uncomfortable with a 'Mills and Boon' love story, you might prefer to consider such feelings as embarrassment, frustration, shame and anger.

I still cringe when I think of the time I dropped a catch on the boundary in a house cricket match. I knew it was a six, and so did the third-formers on the boundary rope, but I swore blind it was only a four. It doesn't matter that Chris Parker won the game off the next delivery, and probably has never given it a second thought. I do and still feel embarrassed by the incident!

A book which lists only successes becomes a total bore and does not ring true. Everybody has some misgivings and failings. It's our flaws that are endearing.

Appealing to the senses

For those not born at the time, it is easy to think of the years before the 1960s as being grey and dull. They weren't ... even though the records we have of that era may be in black and white. Despite the damp day and black and white television pictures, anyone could tell that there was nothing grey about Queen Salote of Tonga at Queen Elizabeth II's Coronation.

Try to recall colours, sounds, textures and smells. You might even be able to capture the bombardment of the taste buds when you tasted foreign food for the first time.

Case study – Monica remembers

Monica knew that she would need a little help in writing her life story. She heard that Sally helped in such projects and felt that sharing the experience would be fun.

At one of their monthly meetings, Sally asked Monica to describe the kitchen in the house in which she first lived. Monica amazed herself at what she recalled – the range, the copper and posser, the mangle and the skiffle board. She even burst into laughter when recalling the sticky fly-papers on the ceiling – after all, Monica later became a health inspector!

Something struck Sally about Monica's reference to the larder. She didn't spot it at first, but then it hit her – Monica sniffed each time she said the word 'larder'. Sally asked Monica to describe the larder. 'There was the slate, the milk jug covered with muslin edged with beads ...' Then it came. Monica told Sally of the net bag hanging on the back of the larder door where her mother kept the meat. She added almost as an afterthought, 'Every time Mum opened the door she sniffed to check that the meat had not gone off.'

Without being aware of it, Monica's sniffing was mimicking her mother's actions all those years ago.

Checklist

- Do you feel comfortable with how you want to come across in the book?
- How much of your life are you prepared to share with your readers?

Assignments

- Think of how you might start your book.
- Over the next few days try to embellish this in your mind.
- Think of the key stories in your life that might warrant similar development.

Tips and Techniques 7

Being aware of writing techniques

The following techniques are often employed by writers. Please feel free to use or discard them as appropriate to the sort of project you have in mind.

Using flashbacks

When writing a chronological life story it can be difficult to deal with everything in order. For example, you may want to include something about your spouse's early life before you met. This is where flashbacks are particularly useful, but it is important to let the reader know what you are doing.

You might want to write something like:

'Before I continue with our married life together, I am going to take a step back to introduce Susan's family and relate something of her early life before we met.'

It will be obvious when the story gets back to the point where you left off. It is then simply a matter of continuing from there.

Using flashbacks for dramatic effect

Flashbacks can also be used to ensure that you don't give the story away too early, thereby losing any potential dramatic effect: 'Everything now all fell into place. I suddenly realised why Bill had been so keen to ensure I brought the camera along ...'

Be careful, though. If flashbacks are used too often they lose their effect and the book can become confusing, not least in knowing what tense to use. If in doubt, keep it simple.

Introducing turning points

In writing a conventional chronological life story, there is little difference between a turning point and a decision. The fact that you were bored with studying and decided to get a job is both a decision and a turning point.

However, if you decide not to write exhaustively about a certain period of your life, your early years for example, the use of turning points can be very effective: 'There were three major turning points in my early life ...'

Turning points are also useful if you include a reflective chapter at the end of your book: 'Looking back I can see that there were five major turning points in my life ...'

Employing cliffhangers

Cliffhangers were regularly used by writers like Dickens whose work appeared in serial form and who needed to keep the reader gripped enough to buy the next issue. Of course, the device is employed by all writers of soaps, and from Saturday morning cinema-going days, many readers will be familiar with 'to be continued ...'

Cliffhangers do not tend to feature significantly in autobiographies. If one does appear at the end of a chapter, the reader simply turns the page to find out more. Greater scope is provided when the cliffhanger is allied with the flashback:

'... so Dick and I married and moved into our idyllic new house, or so we thought. Little did we know what lay around the corner. But before I relate these nightmarish months, I would just like to record something of Dick's early life.'

Creating suspense

Again, with most life stories, there is little scope for high tension, but where there is it is best not to give the game away too early and spoil any potential impact: '... the lady who was to become my wife, give me four wonderful children and with whom I would share 34 blissful years until her untimely death in 1983.' Why bother writing anything more!

The fact that you found a half-brother in later life may be known to most people who will be reading your book, but perhaps not everyone. Learning about the existence of Alf after all those years when you had believed you were an only child came as a tremendous shock to you – why shouldn't it be so for others too? With hindsight, you can appreciate the clues that your mother dropped occasionally, but at the time you thought nothing of them. You might similarly want to drop the occasional ambiguity as readers also like to spot connections.

Case study – Dorothy writes

Having written about her childhood and parents, Dorothy moved on to Chapter 3 of her book:

One day in late spring, when I was 7, Mum took me to one side and told me that I would be going on a journey. It was to be a temporary arrangement while she and Dad settled in America. I was not too worried; to me it was

Case study – Dorothy writes Cont.

going to be a holiday. A gentleman, Mr Jackson, turned up to drive me to my new home where there were lots of other children.

After a few months, Mr Jackson returned. I thought my time had come to go to America, but no, it was not to be. I didn't understand. I asked Mr Jackson why Mum and Dad couldn't take me. Abruptly he told me that my 'Mum' and 'Dad' had only ever been foster parents and that I was an orphan with no relations.

I was devastated. I had had no knowledge of this.

Had Dorothy written: 'Until the age of 7 I was brought up by foster parents who then emigrated to America ...' the impact of her story would have been lost. By writing in this way we can share a little of what Dorothy must have felt at the age of 7.

Talking to the reader

A device some people like to employ is talking to their readers. Care has to be taken if the book is being written for one specific person, like your grandson Peter. Whatever your intentions, the book is likely to be read by others as well, and making the occasional address to 'Peter' might seem exclusive and possibly offensive to others. However, used occasionally in an inclusive manner, it can be effective.

Adding depth to the story

Developing characters

The development of themes can also apply to people. Close friends and family, particularly parents and siblings, are likely to reappear in different chapters throughout the book. Rather than writing everything you know about them when they are first introduced to the story, you might like to develop their characters gradually as the story proceeds. A small anecdote here and an observation there will help the reader to get to know the person better as the writing unfolds, just as you did throughout your life.

Using speech

Speech is perfectly permissible in an autobiography, although overuse can reduce its impact. By reporting speech you have the opportunity of giving depth to the person concerned. To do this, though, the words must be realistic. For example, in speech, most people shorten words: 'do not' becomes 'don't'.

Similarly, speech has to be in character. Someone brimming with anger at having his car boxed in is unlikely to say, 'Excuse me, sir. I would be most grateful if you would be kind enough to move your motor vehicle.'

Embroidering themes within the book

Certain topics, like holidays and hobbies, may well crop up often in your story. For example, if you have been involved in amateur dramatics since childhood you have the choice of writing about it in a single chapter or weaving it throughout your story. The latter is usually preferable as it will include people relevant to different parts of your life. Of course, there's nothing to stop you writing a chapter entitled 'On the Boards' as well as including further references throughout the book.

Knowing how to use conflict

Using conflict points

Classically, conflict is defined in three ways:

- conflict with others
- conflict with nature
- conflict with self.

We tend to think of confrontation when we think of conflict, and often major confrontation at that. This doesn't have to be the case. The Chambers Oxford Dictionary describes conflict as 'to be incompatible'. In effect, it is any area when a decision has to be made. Chocolate or strawberry cheesecake for pudding could fall into this category!

Conflict with others

Best-selling blockbusters thrive on conflict points, and most books on writing encourage the use of this technique for dramatic effect ... and here they do mean serious confrontation. However, with books intended for a private audience it is advisable to play down potentially contentious areas rather than cause friction between friends or within families.

If you are feeling annoyed with someone, be careful what you write. While you are likely to be back on good terms again soon, grievances committed to print are there for posterity.

That is not to say that controversial subjects should not be covered, as can be seen in the next chapter. Further suggestions for writing about difficult areas can also be found in Chapter 11.

Conflict with nature

This category covers all of nature, including the animal kingdom, so your childhood terrorisation by your neighbour's cat is included here.

Stories against nature, like the harsh winter of 1947, London smogs, and falling asleep in the sun and getting terrible sunburn, also feature if they are part of your experience.

Some such stories might have a humorous bent, others may be tragic. They are all part and parcel of life and are to be included.

Conflict with self

Here the opportunities are almost endless – you will be writing about conflict points without even thinking about them.

What might be interesting for you to consider in your book are the times when you struggled over a decision. You can explain how you arrived at your decision and, perhaps with hindsight, whether you feel you made the right choice.

Considering grammar

Writing for a sympathetic audience

Don't get too worked up about your grammar or spelling. This book is intended for a private, sympathetic audience. If you use 'who' instead of 'whom' are your readers really going to throw all your hard work down in disgust? If your grandfather had been guilty of such a heinous crime as a split infinitive would you discard his book in utter derision?

Those writing in longhand can expect assistance in both grammar and spelling if they have the manuscript typed. For those using a word processor, spell check and grammar check facilities will be available. However, be wary of computerised assistance with grammar as the script can become sanitised. Consider using the spell check, but ignore the grammar check and let your character shine through ... even if there is the occasional split infinitive.

More help with grammar will be considered in Chapter 12 at the proofreading stage of the project.

Establishing your house style

All publishers have their own house style to ensure consistency within a book. This covers such areas as when to use upper case letters, numbering systems and punctuation. A few moments thinking about your own guidelines will similarly promote consistency and make for a better book.

The majority of decisions come down to your personal preference.

Using full stops
You were probably taught to use full stops in the following manner:

Dr. Blenkinsop O.B.E., D.F.C. was in the R.A.F.

The current trend is for minimal punctuation, therefore we see:

Dr Blenkinsop OBE, DFC was in the RAF.

Ultimately it does not matter which style you adopt, but sticking to one system will sit more comfortably with your readers.

Dealing with numbers
For consistency and to avoid writing, 'I collected seven thousand, six hundred and twenty-two pennies,' it is worth establishing a numbering system. For example, numbers between one and twelve can be written in words, thereafter digits are used. Exceptions to this are usually:

- dates (14th April)
- years (1962)
- money (£37.23)
- ages ('When I was 7 ...').

Choosing quotation marks
Whether you use double or single inverted commas for speech is up to you. Again, make a decision and stick to it.

Providing emphasis
Some people are very liberal in their use of exclamation marks. Too many can grate and the usual advice is to use only one. If you are particularly flamboyant you may disagree, but please don't bombard your readers with too many!

Similarly, more than one question mark at a time is unnecessary, and any underlining should be used very sparingly, if at all.

Changing font

If your book is to be printed from a word processor, you will probably have the option of changing the style and size of font (lettering, print or typeface). To avoid too many inverted commas, you might consider a different or italicised font for:

- names of pubs – *The Ark*
- book titles – *Writing Your Life Story*
- songs – *The House of the Rising Sun*
- films – *Kind Hearts and Coronets*

Checklist

- Does your story contain any natural moments of suspense?
- Are there any opportunities for employing flashbacks?
- How might conflict be used positively within your writing?

Assignments

- List the turning points in your life and think about how these might be included in your book.
- Write punctuation guidelines for your book.

Inspirational Extracts 8

When writing about your own life, it can be helpful to read books by others who have done likewise. Autobiographies are as popular as ever, so there will be no shortage of choice. In addition to the more high-profile offerings, most libraries and independent bookshops will be able to provide books written by local people. The latter will be particularly helpful, not least because they are more likely to be written by the subject rather than 'with assistance from …'

The object of such reading is to appreciate what is possible, and to assimilate ideas of subject matter and style. Your own style will emerge, just as it does when writing a letter to a friend. You might also gain ideas of how do deal with difficult subjects, which are discussed more fully in Chapter 11.

Interestingly, more can often be learned from a badly written autobiography than a good one. It is important to discover what you don't like, so make a note of anything that grates.

This may include gross exaggeration of events, boasting, or the reverse – which is equally irritating – cloying self-deprecation. Similarly, authors who fall into the trap of 'things aren't as good today as they were in my time' are doing themselves no favours. It is far more effective to explain what life was like – the good and the not so good – and let the readers draw their own conclusions.

This chapter provides extracts from the books of private people, all of whom have written their life stories for family and friends.

A chip off the old block – Olga Moorhouse

Dad always used a safety razor (with Deuce blades) but during the war blades were very scarce, so Dad procured a couple of cut-throat razors which had to be sharpened by stropping them on a large leather belt which hung behind the kitchen door. One day I was drawing and my pencils needed sharpening, so what could be better than the razors! No one would be any the wiser.

I was sitting at the table, using pencils with a beautiful needle-sharp point, oblivious to the fact that Dad had arrived through the back door. 'What the bloody hell!' My blood froze. He stormed into the room brandishing the razors. 'Have you been sharpening your pencils on these?' I put on what I thought was an innocent look. 'What makes you think it was me?' I said. 'Because there are lead marks all across the blades,' he replied, in an ominously low voice, thrusting the objects in question under my nose. I disappeared under the table, which was always my refuge as I could move about under it, and the legs took the brunt of the punishment. He muttered unrepeatable comments on his way back into the kitchen, but I heard one of them! 'She's a bloody little Spitfire that one!'

Incidentally, Olga called her book Bloody Little Spitfire!

A turning point – Peter Deeth

A matter giving me pause for thought was insurance of my flying licence. I was not very keen on insurance in general, but I discovered nearly all the pilots had insured their licences. This meant that if you at any time lost your licence, and therefore your livelihood, perhaps through some illness or an accident, you would at least have something to survive on, or – if you were killed – so would your wife. Of course, I was young and healthy 'and nothing ever happens to me', does it? But we had stringent medicals every six months, and if ever you failed one, you were off flying.

When I joined the company, I had an interview with the personnel officer. He wore a captain's stripes and wings, and I wondered what on earth he was doing in this office job. I happened to glance under the desk on leaving, and saw his legs were in calipers. Polio it was that had laid him low, and there was no vaccine or cure at that time. All this made me think, and I took out insurance. A captain's licence could be covered for £12,000, and this seemed a princely sum to me in those days.

A few weeks later, Peter and I were at the club having a foursome at tennis and a couple of very pretty girls in short shorts were playing on the adjoining court. I was up at the net while Peter served, and at a critical moment I was distracted by the sight of one of the girls bending over to pick up a ball. At that very second, our opponents returned service and the ball came whizzing over the net and caught me right in the eye. My God! I thought I had lost it. The pain was awful. Fortunately, my eye was still there but it became a bloody mess for a few days.

A compulsory six-month medical was coming up, and when the doctor looked in my right eye, he said, 'Holy cow! What have you been doing?' I had a detached retina, and that was that. I was grounded. However, it was only after five weeks in King's College Hospital that it began to dawn on me that perhaps I would never fly again.

This led to a whole new adventure building and running a hotel in Antigua, something which would not have been possible for Peter without the insurance policy... and the two pretty tennis players!

A parent's dilemma – Elizabeth Green

My parents were notified that my school uniform was ready for collection, but so far the allotted grant had not arrived. Until that came, they explained, they just couldn't collect my clothes. The rest of the summer holidays flew by and eventually the last post before the only remaining free day had come, and still no money had been received. That was breaking-point! Most shamefully I admit to showing off quite badly, but in self-defence suggest to feeling very let down and absolutely deflated. The joy and pride of going to my new special school smartly turned out like all the other new girls had disappeared. It was going sadly wrong. 'I'm not starting at the Grammar School in my old clothes! How can I? Now I will never be able to go to that place. Without that lovely uniform, everyone will know we are very poor and will laugh at me,' I sobbed. Following these rather dramatic words came tears of frustration and disappointment. All the pleasure generated by gaining my longed-for scholarship dwindled away. How I must have shattered my harassed parents by this unexpected outburst. I was usually a quiet child.

However, it must have pierced my father's proud and kindly heart and spurred him into action, which was unusual for him as he was such a dreamer. He then did the bravest and most courageous deed I'd ever known him to do. The rates were due, overdue in fact. He had already received the final demand and had planned to send me next day to pay the bill. As usual, there was very little cash in the till and he had no other savings stacked away. Mother's wages had already been used but he had managed during the last few months to put by, bit by bit, the money for that particular account. Instead of asking me to settle the debt, he put on his jacket declaring that he would go to the Town Hall. We were all so amazed as he left Mum and me to look after the shop.

Dad went straight to the tax offices and pleaded my case, saying that he could pay the rates, but that his daughter was starting at the local Grammar School next day, and the promised grant for my uniform had not yet come through. Would they please extend the payment time to allow him to use the rates money to purchase my clothes? He pledged to settle the bill immediately the allowance came through. How he must have hated every minute of that interview, his pride must have been sorely hurt and humbled, yet how much more he must have loved his daughter.

My father was always such a shy, retiring man and was so very downcast by his continual business failures, but he desperately wanted everything right for me. I didn't properly understand the depth of his sacrifice at the time and what it must really have cost him, but I did realise he had been very kind to make that great effort. Now I certainly know what it cost him and I love him more dearly and am eternally grateful.

They did allow him that extra time, and all was well. He returned triumphant, and Mum and I flew to get the uniform. Walthamstow High School, here I come!

Being helpful – Pauline Wakefield

As I had been shown how to use the gas cooker, I thought that I would surprise my parents with breakfast in bed one Sunday morning. I got up quietly and went down to the kitchen, closing the door behind me. I got the tray ready with cups, etc, put the kettle on the stove and got the bread to make toast. All went well – I made the toast, putting some butter in a dish and placing a jar of marmalade on the tray. I also made the tea, remembering to warm the pot first and then putting in the tea leaves (there were no tea bags in those days!). I made my way slowly up the stairs, being careful not to drop the tray.

I think that perhaps Mum may have heard me, but she played the game and feigned surprise when I came in the room. I was pleased that I had done this without any mishaps, and my parents certainly seemed to enjoy their breakfast.

It wasn't till a little later that morning that a problem was discovered. My mother went to make a cup of tea, only to find the kettle on the stove with the gas still on. The kettle had boiled dry… and there was a hole in the bottom! The kettle was one of those with a cap that whistled when the water boiled, and in my desire not to wake my parents I had removed the cap. I had obviously replaced the kettle on the stove, forgetting to turn the gas off. Because of my mistake, I had to buy a new kettle, which seemed a little unfair at the time, especially as I only got 3d (1p) pocket money. I remember that the kettle cost 2/6 (12½p), but I think I only lost two weeks' pocket money before they let me off the rest. However, I am still haunted by this incident whenever I hear a whistling kettle, and I never had one like that myself.

Not making the best of starts – Sir John Quinton

As the new boy, it was my job to take the cheques to the local clearing house in Norwich. During my first week, as I cycled down Guildhall Hill, the wallet containing the cheques fell out of my saddlebag and paper flew everywhere. It says much for the honesty of Norwich people that those who witnessed the catastrophe immediately set to and collected the cheques – so effectively that not one was missing when it came to the exchange. I shudder to think what would have happened if all or even some of them had vanished – Barclays would have had to make good the loss, and my future in the Bank would have been seriously at risk!

John's career was not seriously dented by this incident – he went on to become Chairman!

A *child's perspective – Pat Marriott*

One evening we were waiting for Dad to come home from work when there was a loud knock on the door. I opened the door and a tall policeman stood there. 'Will you fetch your Mummy, please?' he said. Mum must have heard him as she suddenly appeared behind me. 'Go and look after the children,' she said sternly. I slowly walked away into the living room desperately wanting to know what the policeman wanted. The policeman and Mum stood in the hall for some time. He then contacted his office and within a short time some of the family arrived at our house. Mum was crying. She put her coat on and they went out leaving my Auntie with us. No one said anything. I did not know what to think. Where was our Dad? Why didn't he come home?

That night, I went to bed and did not sleep for ages – so many thoughts filling my mind. Somehow I couldn't ask what was wrong. I suppose I didn't want to hear the answer.

The next day we got up and had breakfast, then Auntie Rose and Uncle Fred arrived and then Uncle Alf came, and they all went off to the hospital. Mum had told me earlier that Dad was in hospital after an accident on the road. He was on the back of a motorbike – getting a lift home. A lorry came straight out of a side turning and crashed into the motorbike. Dad got the worst of it. He had bad head injuries, I was told later.

That afternoon when Mum and the family returned, everyone was sad. I could see Mum had been crying, but no one said anything to me. I went out with my friend Noreen, in the garden. She was at my school and lived a few doors down. She asked why I was sad. 'My Dad has died,' I said. Just then a neighbour from upstairs came to the back door and Uncle Fred came out, and I saw him shake his head. I was certain then that my instinct was right.

The next week passed in a blur – people coming and going, and Mum looking so tired. Then one day I was taken to Nan's house. She sat me down and quietly told me all that had happened. Then she said, 'Today, Daddy will be buried.' I let it all out then and cried. At last, someone had told me. I was heartbroken and said, 'I wanted to say goodbye. Why can't I go to the funeral?' Nan replied, 'Mummy thought it was best not to go.'

I know people meant well in trying to avoid the pain for children, but at nine years of age I felt it was better to go through that. Now I know that children must have that choice as they need some sort of closure – a feeling of saying goodbye and letting go. Otherwise, like me, there is no ending. I cannot blame anyone for that. Sadly, it was the way things were done in those days.

Sayings passed into family folklore – Mary Wallwork

My grandfather was the postmaster of Great Barrington and had to deliver telegrams. This was particularly distressing during the war when he had to deliver news of the death of a son or husband. Poor Mrs Soul received five such telegrams during the First World War, each relating to a different son.

Fortunately, there were many lighter moments, and one has passed into our family folklore. A lady in the village, whose daughter Kate was due to visit an aunt in a neighbouring village, needed to pass on the news that Kate would be arriving by bus and not cycling as usual, due to the inclement weather. As telegrams were charged by the word, in an effort to be as concise as possible, my grandfather suggested the wording, 'Kate arriving by bus.' This was unsatisfactory to the lady who wanted to explain why Kate was arriving by bus, even though the neighbouring village would have been experiencing similar weather. The final wording was, 'Simply pouring. Sending Kate by bus.' For years afterwards, whenever it rained, my father would glance out of the window and say, 'My word, Kate will have to go on the bus today!'

Different values – Donna Robertson

I had often imagined myself as a bride, as young girls do, and more so in those days because in most cases living with one's boyfriend was not an option – 'going all the way' was as much frowned upon by one's peers as it was by parents. There was always the fear of pregnancy and being turned out of the house in disgrace, not to mention letting one's parents down or being labelled a slut. However, it was not always easy being so restrained.

I well remember being stranded in Bristol one Friday night; we came out of the cinema to find deep snow and no buses running, certainly not to Axbridge. We managed to find a hotel and booked two single rooms, feeling very guilty and sheepish. We kissed and cuddled good night but didn't dare even to sit on one of the beds. On the Saturday morning, I had to go to work and there was a shocked silence in the office when I walked in – they were amazed to see me there, thinking I'd have been stranded at home. I had to reassure everyone that we had had separate rooms... as indeed we had. I was 19, Kenneth was 29 and we were engaged – it seems unimaginable now.

Unexpected news – Mavis Grant

A few weeks before we left school, we had to take a School Leaving Certificate Exam, and to prove that we were the right age we had to take our birth certificates to the Headmistress, Miss Lowde. Most of the girls had their paper loose in their pockets or satchels, but mine was in a sealed envelope. I didn't attach any significance to this, other than that Mum was being careful, as I had lost things before and she wasn't taking any chances with this item.

When it was my turn to go into her study, Miss Lowde opened the envelope and looked at me as if I had two heads or something, and said, in her most sardonic voice, 'This is not a birth certificate, it is an adoption certificate, but it has your date of birth so will be accepted.'

I was stunned. I had absolutely no idea that I had been adopted. I ran to the toilet and cried my eyes out. I couldn't stop shaking.

One of my classmates saw me, all red-eyed, when I came out and she asked what was the matter. I managed to blurt out my discovery, and she was most sympathetic, saying, 'That's nothing to be ashamed of – I have a cousin who was adopted.' That helped me recover slightly from the shock, but then I started worrying what to say when I went home with the paper.

I went home as usual, handed Mum back the paper, and said nothing as I just didn't know what to say. I continued this choked-up spell of silence, just doing my usual things: playing catch-ball with my doggy pal Tiger, stroking my rabbit, eating my meals in silence and doing my homework before going quietly to bed.

Mum knew there was something wrong, and she worried about it, but I just could not tell her about the shock I'd had at school. However, a few days later, Mum was out when I got home, so I went to see her friend Edith and told her of my dilemma. She kindly offered to tell Mum about it the next day, to which I agreed.

I went home the next afternoon full of apprehension as to how Mum had reacted to the news. I wished I had been able to tell her myself, but as I said, I was going through so many mixed emotions that I just could not find the way to say it.

When I walked in the door, Mum was there alone, crying, which started me off again. Then she cuddled me and said I was never to worry about it again, as she and Dad had really wanted me for their own. She also said that they had hoped I would never know about it, and apart from her own relations and Edith, no one else knew – not that it was anyone else's business anyway. After tea that night, when the boys were out and Dad was shoe-mending in his shed, Mum told me how I came to be their daughter.

I was born prematurely to Alice, aged 17, unmarried, and in what was then known as a workhouse, in Preston, Sussex. I had chronic breathing problems and was not expected to live. I was christened immediately, and as it was May 5th 1926, they named me May. I weighed less than a bag of sugar, Mum said, and a few days after my birth, Alice died. She had afterbirth problems and the nurses thought she had no will to live as her parents had virtually disowned her for committing the cardinal sin of that era by getting pregnant.

After surviving another two weeks, there was a decision to be made as to where I went next. Usually babies were sent to a children's home, but on this occasion, one of the nurses named Viv had an idea which she asked to be considered – would they delay any action until she had contacted her sister? They agreed, and she wrote to her sister Pearl, who had two sons, but who had always wanted a daughter. Pearl became my Mum… I was so lucky.

Love at first sight – Joan Kaemmler

The snow lay deep on the ground as I made my way to the office one morning in January 1947. We were going through the usual ritual of checking our hair and renewing our lipstick when Connie said, 'There are 20 German POWs coming to work in the factory today. Because of the severe weather, there's not enough work for them on the farms.'

When the POWs arrived a little later, we were all standing at a discreet distance from the window as we were very curious to see them – perhaps we were expecting them to be different from us. Behind the German in charge was the most handsome blond man I had ever seen. His brown prisoner-of-war uniform, with patches, was neat and clean, and his trousers were pressed as sharp as a knife. I said to Connie, 'Just look at the blond one in front.' From that moment, my heart belonged to me no longer and I silently marked him as mine. Somehow I knew our destiny was to be together.

Later I discovered his name was Erwin; even the name seemed to have a magical ring about it. I was amazed at my feelings. I was rather a quiet person who usually mistrusted good looks, and yet I knew that this was the man I would share my life with, even though we could not speak a word of each other's language.

Decisive action – Joan Belk

One day, while emptying Arnold's pockets to take his suit to the cleaners, out fell a letter – it was from one of his lady friends. My heart pounded and I went cold inside. I felt bereaved, as if someone had died. In the late '50s, anything like this was shocking.

Still seething inside, I put my coat on and took the bus to Sheffield. As Arnold was at work, I had time on my hands. I found the house and knocked on the door. 'Are you Mrs Jenkins?' I asked. She was, and looked me up and down. 'Do you know Arnold Jackson rather well?' I continued.
'Ye-e-e-s,' she stammered, going quite white.
'Well, I'm Arnold's wife – do you mind if I come inside, or do you want your neighbours to know?'
'Come inside, quick,' she said, ushering me into the house. We sat down and she made some tea. She was so shocked that she trembled – she thought I was going to strike her. I didn't though. I had gone quite cold. I couldn't understand myself.

'Is that your husband?' I said, looking at a large picture of a Navy Officer on the sideboard. She nodded. 'You shouldn't be going out with other women's husbands while he's away at sea. Would you like me to write and tell him what you're up to?' She was a bit stroppy and said, 'You don't know where he is.'

'Oh, but I can soon find out,' I said. 'I've been in the Forces. I'll get in touch with records.' She went white again.

'Please don't,' she pleaded. 'He would stop my allowance at once.'

'Follow me on the next bus down to my house, and I'll forget about it,' I said.

She agreed. Call it blackmail if you like, but I didn't care, the mood I was in.

She did as she promised, and back at the house I gave her a cup of tea. I wasn't nasty – we just chatted amiably.

The door latch went and Arnold came in. He couldn't see her because she was on the settee in front of the fire. This was the moment I had been waiting for. 'Arnold, you have a visitor.' He turned round and saw her. He had such a shock, he was speechless – he knew he'd been caught red-handed. Eventually, all he said was, 'What are you doing here?'

After a difficult conversation and another cup of tea, I said, 'You had better see this lady to the bus.' I was still icy-calm. As soon as he left, I quickly packed his bag, put it outside and bolted the door. When he came back, he pleaded to be let in, but I wouldn't – I put the light out and went to bed. So he slept in the toilet all night, then went down to his mother's in the morning.

* * * * *

More extracts can be found in the companion volume to this book, Times of Our Lives, *which follows a typical life of someone born before or during the Second World War.*

Doing Your Research 9

This chapter will give you an idea of how much research you might like to undertake before you put pen to paper. Some people will be happy simply to record what they remember; others will look to external resources and adopt a more exhaustive approach to their research. The choice is purely an individual one.

You might also like to read the next chapter which considers the process of writing before you return to this chapter and actively work through it.

Glancing through the Appendices is sure to open some memory floodgates, and for those born before 1945, *Times of Our Lives* should prove invaluable, especially in recalling the childhood years. Details can be found under Further Reading at the back of this book.

Being selective

There are an amazing number of sources available to you. What follows is not exhaustive, but hopefully will give you a few ideas. While the emphasis here will be on your early life, the techniques are relevant for the whole project.

Before you go trekking round the country, it is worth looking around your own home. You'll be amazed at what you can remember without even going out of your front door.

Thankfully, the long-term memory appears to get better with age – remembering the name of our first school teacher is often easier than recalling what we had for lunch yesterday.

Prepare for the avalanche of memories!

Mental imaging

Thinking of your childhood home

With a pad of paper and pen to hand, try to picture your childhood home. If you moved house at the age of three or four you will probably want to picture your second home. Essentially, the focus should be on the residence that meant most to you in your early formative years.

Walking round the house

In your mind wander round the house trying to get your bearings and the general layout. If it helps, you might want to sketch a plan of the house noting down details, like who slept in which bedrooms and where the large pieces of furniture were situated.

Walk through the house and up the stairs. You might even remember odd things like the broken banister, how many stairs there were or the colour of that awful wallpaper. Think of the pictures on the walls, the light fittings and ceilings … sticky flypapers and a hole in the ceiling made from your catapult!

Going into the garden

Picture yourself standing in the garden. Was there an outside toilet ... and where did Mum keep the mangle? This might even evoke the memory of your father's pre-Christmas custom of hanging a chicken by its feet in the mangle to drain the blood!

As memories come, jot down notes that you can later weave into stories.

Case study – Ron and June's research

Rather than trusting to memory, Ron decided to phone an estate agent in the town where he grew up. Ron had lived in a long road of 1920s houses and hoped that one might be up for sale. He was unlucky with the first call, but after explaining his quest, the estate agent was able to give him the telephone number of another agent who was selling such a property.

Ron was posted details of the house and with all the dimensions was able to draw an accurate plan. He was amazed how much smaller the house was than how he had remembered it.

June took her assignment a step further and wrote to the tenants at her old address. She received a very warm reply and was invited round for a cup of tea. June's father was a florist and the family of eight children lived above the shop. This had long since been converted into a house and the current owner was delighted to learn how it all pieced together. June spent a wonderfully nostalgic hour or two in her childhood home and now receives the occasional letter bearing her old address.

Refining the research

Try to think of events that took place in each of the rooms – breaking the sitting room window with a tennis ball when playing football in the garden with your brother … it was his fault of course. Mum was particularly annoyed as there was a field the other side of the garden wall and so there was no excuse for playing ball games in the garden!

In your mind, spend time in each of the main rooms of the house: the kitchen, parlour and living rooms particularly.

Case study – George remembers

George shared a room with his older brother Robert. There were twin beds either side of a fireplace; this was never lit unless one of them was ill. George could remember nothing special about the room … except …

Yes … he remembered lying in bed at night and seeing the moon shining though the gaping curtains onto Robert's bed. George was curious. Why did the moon only ever shine on Robert's bed? One night George decided to ask his brother. Robert was 7.

Robert replied, 'The moon only shines on boys who are good.'

George was mortified. Why was only Robert good and not George as well?

A few nights later George woke in the middle of the night … the moon was shining on him. God was saying that George was good.

So special was this memory to George that it was still with him over seventy years later.

Picturing furniture

Even some individual pieces of furniture may reveal a few anecdotes. If only that big old wooden kitchen table covered with the wax cloth could tell a story:

- We ate all our meals round it (no sitting with a tray on our lap watching TV ... there was no TV anyway).
- We did our homework on it ... sometimes.
- It was Mum's sewing table for 'make do and mend'.
- Bill had his head stitched on it.
- Dad plucked the chicken on it at Christmas.
- Scamp saw out his last hours on it before the vet arrived.
- Mum used it for making jam and Dad his homemade wine – Yuk.
- We even hid under it during the air raids.

Don't ignore any room – you might uncover a rare gem, like the antimacassars on the armchairs in the front room that was only ever used on high days and holidays.

Painting character portraits

The way you portray people in your writing will have a large impact on the readability of your book.

Significant people from childhood have helped to shape us and our characters. For example, traits from our parents will be recognisable in ourselves – both the admirable qualities and the frustrating ones! Readers of your book will also recognise those characteristics in you.

Defining the detail

Thinking about the following may help in describing key characters:

- What they looked like.
- What they usually wore ... including the type of hat.

- Mannerisms – Dad's pipe and the nightly ritual in trying to light it.
- Their general disposition: happy, sad, jolly, always singing, whistling, nagging, clicking their fingers …
- What they liked doing to relax.
- Special sayings, like their first words on coming in from outside.
- Their habits.
- How they addressed you.
- How you addressed them.
  etc.

Sketching a brief family tree

Obviously, siblings, parents, grandparents and anyone else who might have lived with you will warrant special attention. To this end, sketching a brief family tree may ensure you don't forget any close relatives – for example, Uncle Jack who stayed with you for a few months after Aunt Maggie died.

Looking at old photos

Rifling through any photograph albums or old pictures stuffed in a shoe box will also stimulate the memory enormously.

These pictures will also remind you of the fashions of the day – describe them.

Incidentally, if there are no names on the back of the photos and you are struggling to remember who everyone is, imagine how much more difficult it will be for those younger than you. Do them a favour and mark the photos accordingly.

Using anecdotes

Try to think of at least one anecdote about each of the main characters from your childhood, about all characters if you can – even the postman with his funny little habit of stopping his whistle mid-flow as he poked the letters through the box, only to start up again from exactly the right point as soon as the letters hit the mat … and the tune was always the same – *The Lambeth Walk*.

Recalling routines

Routines, particularly your mother's, probably dictated much of your childhood existence. Such a routine might have been:

- Monday – wash day
- Tuesday – ironing
- Wednesday – cleaning the house upstairs
- Thursday – baking
- Friday – cleaning the house downstairs.

And there was always shopping to fit in. In the absence of a fridge this may well have involved walking to the shops several times a week.

You might even be able to remember the meals associated with each day's routine.

Then there were the different routines throughout the year:

- jam making
- potato clamping
- rearing day-old chicks
- storing eggs in isinglass
- making wine
- spring cleaning.

Remembering annual events

Annual events will also stimulate dozens of memories, particularly the way you celebrated birthdays and Christmas. Remember, it is often the smallest detail that is the most endearing.

There are likely to have been many other significant days in your calendar:

- Easter
- Empire Day (24 May)
- May Day

- sports day
- end of school
- harvest festival
- Guy Fawkes night
- Christmas pantomime
- carol service.

There may also have been special annual events associated with your town or village:

- an inter-village football match
- church fete
- village fayre
- ox roast
- well dressing.

Using diaries

Any appointment diaries you have kept will be invaluable in jogging your memory. If you also have the type of diary you used to confide in, so much the better, as there will be a wealth of information to draw upon. However, care needs to be exercised. Whilst the diaries of Tony Benn and Kenneth Williams can be reproduced verbatim, most of us do not fall into that category and so the dilemma is how much information to include. Too much detail can be tedious, so it is advisable to read the diaries then put them aside for a few weeks. When you then come to writing about that period of your life, you will remember only the more important episodes to be included.

Of course, certain extracts may make for fascinating reading, like courting days. You could even include a few of the actual entries, like your first thoughts on meeting your future spouse... especially if your impressions were not that favourable! Obviously, how much you are prepared to share with your reader is up to you.

If there is the potential for an imbalance within the book, you could always include a few extracts in the body of the book and then place the rest in an appendix for those who want to read more.

Case study – Living the high life

Ken Robertson was Managing Director of *John Player* for four years during the company's sponsorship of many sporting and cultural events. His wife, Donna, was always in attendance, usually to present trophies, and to 'meet and greet'.

Donna kept a diary during these years, and so when it came to writing her own life story, she had vast quantities of information to draw upon. Rather than bore her readers with dozens of events, Donna listed one year's worth, only expanding upon those occasions where there was an interesting anecdote. She then wrote that the next three years were much the same, to prevent fatigue to her readers.

Describing the neighbourhood

The neighbourhood where you lived as a child was probably your whole world for your first few years. Describing this will create wonderful pictures in the minds of your readers.

Consider walking your reader round the neighbourhood, introducing the main families as you proceed. Explain what sort of town or village it was, where most of the men worked and the type of shops. It might also be significant to note who owned cars in those days.

Then there were the various tradesmen:

- lamplighter
- coalman
- milkman
- the baker's boy
- the grocery boy
- muffin man
- knife sharpener

- Carter Paterson collection & delivery service
- organ grinder
- rag and bone man
- policeman.

Did any of the above have horse-drawn vehicles?

Descriptions of your environment will be all the more important if you lived abroad as a child where the wealth of customs will warrant special attention.

Tapping into the senses

What were the main sounds of your childhood? The siren and the all-clear klaxon during the war ... there were certainly no church bells during the war years as they were only for warning of an invasion. Perhaps other sounds might be associated with the street traders. Was music a feature of your childhood?

Colours were also significant:

- Zebo black lead for the kitchen range
- the donkey stone for the front doorstep
- the smuts from the fireplace
- steam engines spoiling pristine white shirts
- the dull yellow sulphur of the smog.

Smells will also produce memories:

- moth balls
- disinfectants
- Sunlight soap in a solid block
- the gazunder!

Continuing the process

Even these few short pages have probably sent your mind spinning back many years. You can continue with the same techniques to encompass your school days, the church, youth club, etc.

Looking round your house

Your home is likely to be a treasure-trove of memorabilia. Dozens of stories will emerge as you look round each room:

- ✍ ornaments bought on holiday or given by special friends long since gone
- ✍ messages in the front of books kept since childhood
- ✍ your father's fob watch presented to him after 25 years at the bank.

The attic should not be forgotten either – this is where some of the best material may be found ... old school reports, 78 rpm gramophone records, etc.

You might want to take some of the smaller items of memorabilia to your special writing area. Certain photographs are likely to be required for the final production and you may want to store these together. As they will be out of circulation for some months, you may prefer to make notes referring to the photos in question rather than removing them from walls and shelves all over your home. If you are planning a surprise book, the absence of special photos in the house will be a give-away.

Those proficient with a scanner can scan the photos and other documents in readiness for the final book. (See Chapter 17 for further details.) The back-up procedures outlined earlier should also be adopted.

Including everything
Don't forget to take your note pad with you as you look at such things as:

- ✍ framed photographs
- ✍ pictures on the wall
- ✍ bric-à-brac
- ✍ books
- ✍ ornaments
- ✍ jewellery

- old greetings cards
- documents
- certificates
- school reports
- gramophone records
- old toys
- dried flowers
- your wedding dress.

You may also have an old family Bible containing a record of family names and important dates.

Let your imagination roam, and take your time ... you are likely to experience many different emotions.

Enlisting the help of others

Reminiscing with friends

You might like to discuss particular ideas with friends or perhaps your partner. One thing will lead to another and, before you know it, a further chapter is in the making.

Asking elderly relatives

As with genealogy, it is essential to pursue lines of enquiry currently available but which may disappear imminently. Older relatives might be able to provide details you never knew about your parents, furnishing you with fantastic new material for your book.

Many of us have intriguing snippets wallowing in the recesses of our minds – maybe something mentioned in passing when we were younger, a slip of the tongue followed by a contrived change of subject, or perhaps the abrupt termination of a conversation when we came into the room. Older friends and relatives might be able to shed light on such mysteries, being willing to open up now that the passage of years has diffused the impact of any skeletons in the cupboard.

If you talk to someone who remembers older members of the family, once you have asked about any intriguing matters, don't forget to quiz them about more mundane, potentially frivolous details – perhaps what your grandmother looked like, any mannerisms, favourite sayings, accidents and the like. Also ask for anecdotes, as these can provide fascinating insights, an off-the-cuff remark leading to some real gems.

Of course, if you are the oldest member of the family your recollections are the ones to be captured. By all means undertake wider research later, but if you are the source of any unique information, the advice here is to record that first. Records in the public domain are likely to be available once you have preserved your own memories, but it would be a shame for future generations to miss out on your own pearls of wisdom.

Carrying out wider research

You may feel that you have enough information for your purposes already without undertaking any wider research. However, if you want greater stimulation, there is plenty at hand.

Making use of the library
You may have plenty of reference books at home, but the local library will offer many more tempting opportunities.

Q: Are there any books in particular that you would recommend?

A: There are many excellent reference books available. However, one stands head and shoulders above the rest, *Dorling Kindersley's Chronicle of the 20th Century*.

Featuring one month per page, this huge tome trawls through the twentieth century. As each page bears a date, you can work out how old you were and place events accurately within your story. The book also contains many pictures, and in addition to reminding you of all major world events, you can see who won Wimbledon, changes in fashion and relive the hit songs and films of the year.

Despite being out of print, copies can often be obtained from secondhand bookshops, and they also occasionally turn up in charity shops.

Watching videos and films

Videos can provide a wealth of information, especially those that focus on a particular year. It might be worth watching the videos of some of the key years in your life to help get into the mood and to remind you of the social history.

Remembering the big films of that era will also help. You might recall where you first saw Disney's *Snow White* or *Gone with the Wind* and who you went with.

Listening to music and nostalgic tapes

Whether your idol was Frank Sinatra, Deanna Durbin or Bill Haley, certain songs will undoubtedly evoke particular memories.

Nostalgia tapes are also available of such classics as *Round the Horne*, *The Goons* and *Dick Barton, Special Agent*. Memories will pour forth when listening to these, and they may also have been the catalyst for in-jokes and family sayings. Alternatively they may have been the cause of family conflict if you were not allowed to listen to such programmes as *Valentine Dyall – The Man in Black*, yet your school friends were!

Reading specialist magazines

There are many nostalgia magazines available:

- *Yours*
- *Evergreen*
- *Best of British*
- *Goodtimes*
- *Saga*
  etc.

Service magazines might also be of help, as well as specialist organisations like *The Overseas Pensioner Association* for those who worked abroad.

Visiting museums

There are dozens of fabulous nostalgia museums that will send your memory reeling back to your childhood. Your nearest tourist information office and library will provide details of those in your area.

For those who want a trip to London, the Museum of Brands, Packaging and Advertising will not disappoint. You will see the packaging of hundreds of products from your childhood:

- *Reckitt's blue*
- *Robin Starch*
- *Strand cigarettes*
- *Beechams pills*
- *cod liver oil*

 … the list is endless.

St Fagan's near Cardiff is also worth a visit. Its row of cottages furnished in different periods throughout the twentieth century is particularly fascinating. Beamish Open Air Museum in County Durham and Bethnal Green Museum of Childhood are also excellent.

There are war museums like the Cabinet War Rooms, the Imperial War Museum, Bletchley Park, etc., as well as dozens of aviation, naval and army museums.

Seeking old friends

Many nostalgia and service magazines host a 'Where are they now?' column for old friends trying to get back in contact. The same is available for those with access to the Internet, via friendsreunited.com. This website lists tens of thousands of schools and workplaces and is an excellent way of finding details about, and contacting, old friends and colleagues.

Taking that extra step

The above list should provide ample scope for most people, but those looking for specialist information can refer to local and national records offices.

Another source worthy of consideration for the more enthusiastic researcher is the National Newspaper Library in Colindale, London N11. Here you can read through local and national newspapers from decades ago. It is a fascinating place, but worth booking first.

Incorporating social history

Weaving in the detail

It is important to try to encapsulate your childhood for grandchildren who have never known anything but colour TV, trainers, mobile phones, fast food restaurants and computers.

Some events will be included because of their significance in your life, like the war, rationing and going to an Adam Faith concert. Other details will be added for social background, like your encounter with American GIs who were 'overpaid, oversexed and over here'!

Tying in important dates

Certain events in history are momentous and we can picture where we were when we heard the news. Depending on your age, events that you might want to consider include:

    the outbreak of the Second World War

    VE Day and VJ Day

    the death of King George VI

    the Coronation of Queen Elizabeth II

    Roger Bannister breaking the four-minute mile

    John F. Kennedy being shot

    Winston Churchill's death and funeral

    man landing on the moon.

Considering more ideas

For those still not satisfied that they have enough information, here are a few more ideas you might like to ponder:

    Why I was given my name …

    Stories I know about my birth …

    A day in the life of my mum; A day in the life of my dad (at the weekend maybe) …

    A typical week in my childhood …

    The importance of religion in my childhood …

    Childhood illnesses …

    Hospital visits as a child …

      – stitches …

      – something stuck up my nose …

    Things I broke:

      – my Mum's favourite vase …

      – my leg …

      – my brother's leg …

      – my heart when Granny died …

    The street traders of my childhood …

    My favourite toy …

    Family jokes; Family sayings; Family traditions …

    My first taste of foreign food …

    My first trip to London …

    Why I was caned; Why I was not caned …

    My favourite teacher …

    My best sporting moment; My worst sporting moment …

    The five things which have given me the greatest satisfaction …

- My proudest moment when I was 10 (or thereabouts); My proudest moment in my teens ...
- When I felt most:
  - frightened ...
  - elated ...
  - triumphant ...
  - content ...
  - ridiculous ...
  - embarrassed ...
- What I most regret ...
- The day my world fell apart ...
- Different houses in which I've lived ...
- The jobs I've had ...
- Countries I have visited ...
- My ten most memorable holidays ...
- Pets we have had ...
- I remember seeing my first:
  - hair dryer ...
  - refrigerator ...
  - radiator ...
  - electric cooker ...
  - television set ...
- I remember first travelling:
  - in a car ...
  - in a train ...
  - in an aeroplane ...
- Five 'what ifs' in my life ...
- My ten best decisions; My ten worst decisions ...
- Opportunities – taken and not taken ...
  etc.

Checklist

- Who were the important people in your childhood?
- How much social history do you want to include?
- What wider research do you want to undertake?
- Refer to the listings at the back of the book.

Assignments

- ✍ Decide which day trips you might like to go on.
- ✍ Research which magazines might be useful.
- ✍ In the light of this chapter and the final list of ideas, review what insights you wish to share with your readers.
- ✍ Get hold of *Times of Our Lives* from the library and try to locate a copy of *Chronicle of the Twentieth Century*.

Being Ready to Write

10

Having planned the structure of your book, considered various writing techniques and looked at dozens of research ideas, you are now almost ready to start writing.

All that remains to do is:

- Decide the chapter where you want to begin writing.
- Review the chapter plan.
- Immerse yourself in memories.
- Revise the chapter plan.
- Get writing!

Deciding where to start writing

By now you will have given some thought to where you want your book to begin. For most people this will be with what they know of their immediate forebears, or with their own childhood.

Just because the book might start with childhood, it does not follow that you have to write this chapter first. If you had a difficult childhood, for example, you may prefer to write about something else initially – maybe your first job or a holiday. You can always come back to your childhood once you are into the flow of writing.

The most difficult part of the process is putting pen to paper, so it is important that you begin your writing wherever you feel comfortable.

For convenience here it shall be assumed that the book begins at childhood.

Reviewing the chapter plan

In Chapter 4 we looked at the structure of the book, breaking it down into various chapter headings. The more thorough you were then, the easier the next step will be.

Select the chapter where you want to start writing and review what you wrote under that heading. The aim here is to think along similar lines as when you wrote those notes.

Immersing yourself in memories

Essentially, you want to become immersed in that period of your history about which you are writing. All we are doing now is following the same techniques as before, but in greater detail.

In this you may be helped by:

- introducing year sheets
- familiarising yourself with the history of the period
- being prepared for the avalanche of memories.

Introducing year sheets

Time lines were considered when structuring the book. Year sheets follow the same principle but provide greater detail.

Assuming that you were born in 1930 and that you are focusing on your childhood, you would entitle sheets with the years from 1930 to 1945, one year per sheet. It helps to write how old you were alongside the year. By having separate sheets you can add any extra when necessary.

Dates worth recording might be when you started or changed schools. In this particular example the war will obviously feature as well. Of course, the two subjects will merge. Your twelfth birthday might be memorable because your party was celebrated in the Anderson shelter... and it was a very small birthday cake thanks to rationing!

Write down any memories relating to each year. It will be difficult to be precise, particularly in the first few years, but try to include any interesting anecdotes relating to that general period in your life.

Dealing with overlaps

Such an extensive period is likely to cover several chapters:

- meet the family
- our neighbourhood
- childhood
- school days
- evacuation
- the war years.

This is inevitable with the early years where much of the information interlinks. While some topics will overlap chapters, it should be fairly logical where most stories belong.

Coloured highlighter pens are useful to link notes on your year sheets with the different chapters.

Familiarising yourself with history

A brief review of the period of history about which you are writing will open up many more ideas. It will also help you to be more specific about where anecdotes fit with the time sheets.

Social history is particularly important in these early chapters, but where your early years coincide with world events (like the Second World War), you will also want to weave them into your story. What you witnessed of such events will be of particular interest, maybe watching a dogfight or being frightened by a doodlebug.

Coping with the avalanche of ideas

As before, organisation is vital. All sorts of random recollections will come to you and it is important that none are lost, so have plenty of paper to hand, not just for the chapter in question, but for others as well.

Revising the chapter plan

You are likely to have pages full of random memories. You can now connect all the similar ideas and rewrite them in some semblance of order. This is very much like the process undertaken in structuring the book.

Much of the information on different year sheets will be related and you will want to group these subjects together rather than write rigidly in years.

If you have masses of information you can divide the chapter. That's fine, but don't worry unduly – the chapter can always be divided at the review stage if you feel uncomfortable with it at that time.

Allowing thinking time

The subconscious is amazing. Once you delve back in time all sorts of memories will flash into your mind, often when you are least expecting them. Allow time to sift and develop ideas.

Settling on your chapter plan

Sooner or later, maybe after many revisions, you will be happy with your chapter plan. This will provide you with a sequence of the subjects to be covered and in which order.

Sitting down to write

By the time you sit down to write you should be in the following position:

- have a planned structure for your book
- know at what point you want to start your writing
- have a detailed chapter plan
- feel comfortable with the amount of research you have undertaken
- have given special thought to the opening.

Keeping it simple

All you are trying to do is communicate your story. You speak fluently without deliberating over every word – write in the same uncomplicated way.

Try to keep your writing simple, and don't be tempted to rush to the dictionary and thesaurus every few sentences. Use your own vocabulary and enjoy what you are doing – just like writing a letter to a friend.

Write several pages in one sitting and don't be tempted to reread every paragraph before moving on to the next. You want the writing to flow.

When you reread a section you will probably want to fine-tune it a little. However, don't be too critical at this stage – that comes when you revise the book. What you are looking to do here is get several pages under your belt to boost your confidence.

Allowing for deviation

Even while you are writing you are likely to think of other ideas. If the memories are about a topic not yet touched upon, simply jot notes on your chapter plan to develop later.

Additional recollections concerning a subject about which you have already written can be accommodated by inserting a page at the appropriate place, as discussed in Chapter 3.

Understanding the challenge of the early chapter

Having written the first chapter you are well into the project and nothing should stop you now. If your first chapter is about your childhood you can be doubly pleased – it tends to be one of the more complex because of all the different subjects to introduce. Later chapters usually flow chronologically with fewer topics competing for attention.

Revising provisional targets

Having written one chapter you will have a greater understanding of what is involved and how you work.

If the timescale for the project is an important consideration you might want to revise it. An unrealistic schedule might lead to disillusionment. It is better that you feel comfortable in undertaking a more modest project, or extend the anticipated timescale, rather than give up in frustration.

This is meant to be an enjoyable hobby. It is therefore important that you don't put yourself under too much pressure and resent ever having begun.

Continuing the process

Keep on writing

Essentially all you need do now is follow the same steps as before. It's that simple!

Invariably when writing some of the later chapters you will think of additional memories for inclusion earlier in the manuscript. Tying these memories into the relevant chapter is satisfying as it makes for a more thorough book. This process is likely to continue right up to the time the book is bound ... and even then you will think of things you have forgotten!

Q: I seem to be writing a great deal about my early life. Is it too detailed? I know I won't have so much material later.

A: Most family-centred books tend to be weighted in favour of the early years, and perhaps two-thirds of the writing will cover the first 30 years or so. This is not unusual – after all, this period of your life involves more scene-setting.

If you have had an extensive career, a diverse life, or if there is a particular focus to your middle or later years, the balance of your book will be more even. However, avoid the mistake of skipping over your formative years, which will be of great interest to your readers, especially family.

Dealing with writer's block

Hopefully you will enjoy your writing. However, even if you are highly motivated there may come a time when the words do not flow so easily. If you find yourself in that position, here are some techniques you might like to consider.

Being disciplined

Most writers agree that there is no substitute for discipline. When their livelihood depends on what they produce they just have to persevere. Thankfully, you are not in such a position. This project is intended to be enjoyable and it is hoped that some of the following methods will be more appealing.

Creating routines

Some people are most inspired at a certain time of day. Alternatively, there might be a day of the week when everyone is out and you know you won't be disturbed. If you recognise such patterns, use them to your advantage.

Setting realistic targets

If you are feeling a little daunted by the size of the project ahead, make sure that you focus only on smaller tasks like topics within individual chapters.

Don't set yourself too great a target like writing for five hours at a stretch. Even twenty minutes can be very productive and might help you through a difficult patch. You may then feel inspired to spend longer next time.

Leaving off in mid-flow

It is good to leave a session of writing wanting to write more. In recognition of this, some writers even stop a paragraph or sentence in mid-flow so they can pick it up next time.

If you don't like this approach, you may at least want to leave a stimulating topic to start with at the next session.

Reading

Rereading what you wrote last time is an excellent way of getting back into your stride. Alternatively, you might want to review your chapter plan.

If inspiration is still not coming, you can try reading the intro-duction explaining why you wanted to write in the first place.

Reading another autobiography can also be helpful in trigger-ing ideas ... as long as you don't become too engrossed and spend the whole afternoon on that book!

Being constructive

If you don't feel like writing, you can use your time construc-tively in other ways:

- ✍ reviewing the book structure
- ✍ revising the chapter plan
- ✍ brainstorming another chapter
- ✍ reading history or reference books
- ✍ doing some other research
- ✍ thinking
- ✍ planning the book launch!

Imposing a deadline

If all else fails, you might want to impose some deadlines on yourself. This is particularly effective when you make a com-mitment to someone else. If you tell a friend that you would like to send a chapter at the end of the month for review you will feel a responsibility to get the chapter written.

A writing circle or external writing partner fulfils a similar dis-cipline for those who never completed their homework until the night before it had to be handed in!

Case study – Shirley's SFNs

Shirley was enjoying writing her life story, but she found it difficult to get started. Sitting down at the typewriter was no problem, but getting into the flow was not so easy until Shirley developed her own special technique.

Case study – Shirley's SFNs continued

Before continuing with her life story, whenever Shirley sat down to write she typed two or three paragraphs about the few days since her last session. She might include frustrations with the washing machine repairman or the wonders of modern supermarkets. Whatever it was, it got Shirley into a writing frame of mind and she then found it easy to turn her attention to her 'real writing'.

Although obviously not included within the book, 'Shirley's famous notes' as they became known, formed a fascinating record in their own right. Incidentally, since completing her book Shirley has started a diary.

Checklist

- Where do you want to start writing?
- Are you fully prepared?
- How might you deal with writer's block?

Assignments

- Prepare a chapter plan for your first chapter.
- Write your first chapter.
- Revise any provisional targets you set for writing your life story.

Tackling Difficult Areas 11

You might encounter some difficulties in writing your life story. This chapter will help deal with such areas.

Ultimately, this is your book...only write what you feel comfortable about.

Thinking about yourself

Being emotionally prepared
A vast array of memories will flood forth as you reflect over your life. While this is likely to be a hugely enjoyable process, you may also encounter some painful emotions. When you know that you are coming to such a stage in your story, allow yourself the space you need to be emotionally prepared.

The death of a loved one may well fall into this category. Writing can be cathartic, and you will also have the opportunity to pay tribute to this special person in your book, but it is worth being prepared before you open up any painful memories.

Allowing a passage of time

Writing about the war can similarly produce powerful emotions and it sometimes takes 30, 40, 50 years or more before these memories can be reviewed. Some people find that they can never write about such times.

If you decide to include painful memories you might be deflected in your desire to finish the rest of your story. It is therefore advisable to have an easier chapter lined up to get back into the flow after you have written about a traumatic event.

Case study – David's honesty

David was progressing well with his writing, but there was a period looming that he did not know how to handle. It covered five years in his life when things were difficult, both with his career and domestically. He did not want to hurt his wife or children by what he wrote.

David had the choice of fudging over these five years – after all, there was no need to describe them in detail, and with a bit of creative wording he knew that most readers would be none the wiser. However, David wanted to acknowledge that he'd had problems without going into any details – he didn't know how much he'd be able to remember anyway.

In the end, David wrote the following: 'I found the next five years of my life very difficult. I don't know if I cannot or do not want to remember them, but I am moving on in my story to ... '

Deciding what to include

Knowing who to mention
Most of the people to be mentioned in your book will have been highlighted in the various chapter plans, but it is worth ensuring that significant people have not been omitted.

Those likely to be reading your book
You probably feel that you can name all those who will be reading your book – the list may be longer than you envisage. Once people hear that you have written a book, you will be surprised who might ask to borrow a copy: neighbours, friends from the bowls club or church, old work colleagues, etc.

You might like to include something along the lines of:

> 'For the last few years Betty and I have been members of the local social club. Jean and John, Fred and Jill, Max, Bob and Wilf have all been good friends and we look forward to our monthly get-togethers.'

They will be delighted to be included in your book, and it may well save you a little embarrassment when they ask to borrow a copy.

The Christmas card list is also likely to reveal both names and anecdotes for inclusion in your book.

Trawling through your address book (and any old ones you can find) will provide another fertile source of potential readers and memories.

Writing about the family
If you have children, knowing how much to include about them will partly depend on the intended audience for your book. As a general rule, it is reasonable to include a few anecdotes about them until they left home, thereafter you will

probably just cover the main events in their life: career, marriage, house moves and any grandchildren. This follows the assumption that the book is about your life not theirs, and that if they want to write their own book in future years, that is their prerogative.

Being even-handed

For the sake of family harmony, it is important to be even-handed when mentioning any children and grandchildren. There may be more to write about the oldest grandchild, but the others warrant their share of attention. While favouritism is not intended, it can be perceived.

Using in-jokes

In-jokes are fine – after all this is a family book. Some family jokes will go over the heads of many readers. That is acceptable if the reference is not obvious. Where the reference is obvious, you may have to explain the point so that others can also share the fun.

Deciding what not to include

Dealing with libel

Libel is defined as writing something that will damage a person's reputation or their livelihood. Even if you know what you write is true, you have to be able to prove it. Any court proceedings are likely to be emotionally traumatic and financially ruinous.

Even changing the name of the person will not get you off the hook if they can reasonably be identified by your writing.

The simple advice here is to steer clear of anything that is libellous or potentially libellous. If you feel that badly towards someone, why even give them the satisfaction of a mention in your book?

If it is a subject of great importance to you, at least try to be balanced and present the other point of view – even if you do not agree with it. Remember, if you write anything vitriolic, it is likely to say more about you than the other person!

Handling relationships
You need to be diplomatic if writing about past relationships.

Writing about divorce
If writing about your own divorce, the safe option is to say little. There will be your ex-partner, as well as perhaps a current partner and any children to consider. Something non-controversial like, 'Sadly, the marriage did not work out,' is a safe approach, although one lady preferred to write: 'Fred looked good in his police uniform – it's just a shame that other women thought so as well!' As was seen in Chapter 8, Joan Belk took a tougher line, although she did change the name of the lady concerned. Ultimately, such decisions have to be yours.

If the divorce relates to another couple, maybe involving a child or sibling, question why the information needs to be included. If it does, avoid detail and consider checking your provisional writing with the parties concerned.

Writing about old flames
Again, if the subject is likely to be contentious, think twice. Ask yourself what is to be gained by including the information and who might find it difficult to read. Your partner may find it insensitive if you write in detail about old flames. If you decide to proceed, it might be worth seeking your partner's approval over the wording before it appears in the final book.

Relationships that are further afield, maybe concerning children, have less of a part in your book. If they want to write about them in future years that is up to them. If they are happy for you to include details, be sensitive.

Case study – Helen writes creatively

Helen had got to the stage in her story when she was going to write about her daughter, Jane. On leaving university, Jane went to work in France where she shared a flat with her boyfriend, Steve. Helen wrote, 'When Jane got the opportunity to go to France, she needed no second invitation. Once in Lyon, Jane began to teach English at a language school, sharing a small apartment with her boyfriend, Steve.'

Helen asked her daughter about this wording; Jane was happy with it, even though she is now married to Paul and they have four children. Helen still felt a little uncomfortable and in the end wrote, 'Once in Lyon, Jane began to teach English at a language school, sharing a small apartment with a friend.' Helen felt that if Jane wanted to write her own book in years to come and mention Steve, that was up to her.

Getting things off your chest

Words said in jest down the pub might not look quite so funny when printed in a book. Just because you have written something does not mean that it has to appear in the final presentation. The very process of writing may have served the purpose of getting it off your chest.

Dealing with sex and colourful language

While blockbusters may be sprinkled liberally with sex and colourful language autobiographies intended for friends and family rarely fall into the same category.

Whilst the advice is not to offend loved ones, they know you and would feel cheated if interesting stories were omitted.

Case study – Joan Belk included the following in her book

Trade at the shop was slow on Mondays and I was skint, so one night at home I said to Albert, 'Do you know where I can get a gross of Durex from?' His eyebrows shot up and he smiled. 'And what are you going to do with a gross of Durex?' 'Leave it to me,' I replied.

The next day Albert trotted down town and came back with a box under his arm. 'You've got a discount on them as you are trade – aren't you the lucky one?' He still didn't ask me what I was going to do with them. He just smiled. Curiosity would have killed me!

I had put an advert in the *Rotherham Advertiser*, 'Durex 4 Pkts 10/- under plain wrapper, first class stamp, swift delivery,' together with my address. There it was in print, very nice. I asked Pauline to fetch me a bundle of brown envelopes and 50 first-class stamps, and then we waited for Monday morning. Don't forget we had a good postal service in those days.

Monday morning came, and so did the postman. He emptied nearly half a bag of envelopes. 'Somebody's birthday, Joan?' 'No,' I answered, 'just business.' Pauline and I looked in amazement and were very excited. As we emptied them, out came ten-shilling notes and pound notes. This became quite a routine over the years, a few coming in during the week, but the bulk coming in on Monday mornings. It was ideal for us, and a nice little earner.

Getting the facts right

Remembering major historical dates

Most dates can be easily checked in reference books. If you can't find a precise date, the month and year, or just the year, will suffice. If you get the date wrong, someone might notice, but it is not going to cause offence.

Remembering significant family dates

The dates of birthdays and anniversaries are likely to be of greater importance than national milestones – at least, the consequences of getting them wrong will be more significant! Writing that Queen Elizabeth II's coronation was in 1952, and not 1953, will not get you locked up in the Tower, but getting your grandson's date of birth wrong is likely to have consequences ... if not from him, then from his parents! It really is worth checking these facts thoroughly. The last thing you want to do is cause offence.

Checking the spelling of names

The same holds true for names as it does for dates. If Rachmaninov is spelt 'Rachmaninof' you are unlikely to face many repercussions. Spelling a grandchild's name incorrectly is a different matter. Again, check thoroughly.

Ending the book

Knowing where to finish

If you set out with the intention of writing about a certain period of your life, the ending of the book will be obvious: when you were demobbed or when you retired maybe.

Using a milestone

In writing a full autobiography it is likely that you will want to bring the narrative up to date. Rather than let the writing trail off, you might find it easier to close at an appropriate milestone. This might be:

- your 75th birthday
- completing your year as captain at the bowls club
- your 47th wedding anniversary
- the birth of your latest grandchild or great niece
- the Millennium, or the new year of 2005 ... 2006 ...
- the cruise to Madeira
- a reunion.

Finishing positively

Readers like to feel uplifted at the end of a book. You might want to consider looking to the future … 'As this book draws to a close I look forward to catching up with all my other hobbies and, who knows, in 15 years' time I may have to consider a sequel!'

Bringing a smile to the face of the reader

If it is your style, you might consider ending on a humorous note. One author concluded his magnum opus with the imaginary scene of reading his book to his grandson:

> 'That's enough. We close the book now and you must go to sleep and dream.'
> 'Goodnight, Granddad.'
> 'Goodnight.'
> 'Oh, Granddad?'
> 'Yes?'
> 'Granddad, will you leave your book?'
>
> With pride swelling in my chest I leave the book on Tom's bedside table.
>
> 'Thanks Granddad.'
> 'Do you want to read it in the morning?' I ask.
> 'No. But if I stand on it, I can reach the top of the cupboard.'

Writing a summary

Having completed their manuscript, some people like to review their life, reflecting on the changes they have witnessed and the people they have met.

Checklist

- What areas of your life do you not want to share?
- Is there anything in your book which is potentially libellous?
- Is anyone likely to be offended by what you include? If so, does it need to be in your book?

Assignments

- Write a list of the people who might conceivably read your book.
- Check important family dates and the spelling of names.
- Consider how you might end your writing.

Revising the Manuscript

12

A few hours spent revising your manuscript will reap rewards disproportionate to the effort expended. We all make mistakes, but the majority of these can be corrected with a thorough review.

In revising your manuscript there are three main areas to consider:

    & the structure and style
    & the content
    & the grammar.

You should be able to consider all of the above areas in one reading, especially if an independent proofreading is being considered – more of which later in the chapter.

Taking a break

Once you have written your manuscript it is worth taking a break to allow a certain distance and objectivity for when you review your writing. Having just completed the book your mind is likely to be too cluttered to be able to look at the overall structure in a detached manner.

If you feel that getting out of the habit of working on your book will be counter-productive, you can always spend the time sorting any photographs to be included or perhaps planning how the book is to be launched.

Revising the structure and style

The idea of this part of the review is to ensure that the manuscript is well structured and that the story flows smoothly.

Starting with the introduction

In reading the introduction you will remind yourself of the purpose for writing the book and, perhaps, what you intended to include. If the final manuscript has deviated from these original intentions, or if there is anything else you would like to add as a result of writing, simply amend the introduction.

Reviewing the first chapter

The first chapter was probably written many months before the final one, during which time your style is likely to have changed. It sometimes takes a chapter or two to find your writing voice, something which sits more comfortably when the project is underway. Additionally, the early chapters often contain fewer insights as the author establishes how much detail should be included. As a result, some people choose to rewrite, or at least elaborate upon, the first chapter.

Proceeding a chapter at a time

There is no ideal length for a chapter, but try not to make it too long. A useful rule of thumb is to read through a chapter in one sitting and see if it feels comfortable. It may be that you want to divide a chapter and can spot an appropriate place. Alternatively, you might want to join two or three short chapters together.

As chapters often have an introduction and a conclusion, any restructuring may result in having to refine a few sentences.

Finalising the chapter headings

Chapter headings are not essential, although they serve to tell the reader what lies ahead. Hopefully they are also of some assistance in the writing of the book, and the use of them is encouraged if you have no strong views to the contrary.

In life stories chapter headings usually run along the lines of:

- Meet the Family
- Early Years
- School Days.

These are perfectly adequate, although it is worth avoiding the overuse of words like 'years' – 'Early Years', School Years', 'War Years', etc. – unless you are deliberately seeking symmetry.

Thinking laterally about chapter headings

You can be more creative in your use of chapter headings if that is your style.

- a quotation
- something intriguing
- a verse from the Bible
- a stanza of your own poetry
- a song title
- some Latin.

Of course, you can also have a chapter heading followed by a quotation or verse as a sub-heading.

Revising the content

Identifying structural imbalance

Having taken a break you will be in a better position to look at the overall structure of the book. Any glaring imbalance should be obvious.

It may be that you decided to include your childhood diary in the first chapter of your book. You now appreciate that 27 pages was a little too long and this has created an imbalance in the book. Rather than discard such valuable information, consider including the diary as an appendix, perhaps keeping two or three pages in the first chapter.

The appendix can be a wonderful depository for any information that would otherwise create an imbalance in the book.

Looking for omissions

Having taken a break you will be in a better position to spot any omissions – a common problem when you are so familiar with the story.

For example, your brother Jeremy was obviously introduced in your childhood chapter, but now you notice that you made no reference to his wife Claire. And this is despite the fact that you were Jeremy's best man and the wedding was an unforgettable occasion!

Checking against a list of names

To ensure that you have not omitted any significant people, before you review the manuscript write an exhaustive list of names of those who should feature in your story. Particularly useful are:

- Christmas card lists and address books
- photograph albums
- family tree
- lists of those likely to read the book.

As you read through the manuscript tick off the names as they are mentioned. If you have chatted to friends about your book, it is all too easy to think that you have recorded a story when in fact you have only talked about it.

Maintaining harmonious relations

If your manuscript is on a word processor it can be useful to check the number of times each child and grandchild has been mentioned, especially if there is potential for family rivalry.

Case study – Betty's favouritism

Betty, a widow, had always wanted to write a book and decided that her eightieth birthday would be the perfect occasion to present it to her three children, Mark, Paula and Sarah. Being very organised, Betty started writing eighteen months before the intended milestone and made good progress. Towards the end of the project, she enlisted help to edit the book and produce a few presentation volumes.

Whilst reviewing the manuscript, it became obvious to the assistant that more had been written about Sarah than the older children. A simple search of the three names revealed that indeed 'Sarah' appeared nine times more often than either 'Mark' or 'Paula'. Betty could readily point to reasons why this should be so, but fortunately there was time to redress the balance in the writing before potential problems occurred – the photographs were revised accordingly. All three children were delighted with the book on Betty's eightieth birthday.

Spotting duplications

As your writing will have been undertaken over a long period of time, it is not uncommon to find that you have written about the same event twice. If you review the whole manuscript in a relatively short period, such duplication should jump out at you.

Eliminating excessive material

On rereading your manuscript you may decide that some details are superfluous, that you got a bit too carried away. Only you can be the judge of this, but prune sparingly and avoid discarding any real treasures. As has been stated before, the fact that you remembered these details from maybe 50 or more years ago must mean something. What would you cut from your grandmother's book if you were given the choice?

Correcting continuity errors

It is worth being on your guard for continuity errors. For example, if you mention your nephew before writing about your sister even meeting, let alone marrying, her husband, the reader may be justifiably confused.

Case study – Jack's fit of pique

Jack was feeling a bit fed up. He had intended to get down to his writing straight after lunch, but then Harry turned up and proceeded to tell him all about the problems on the allotment ... it was not as if Jack had not heard them a dozen times before.

It just so happened that Jack was up to the point in his story when he and Sheila went on holiday with Harry and Vera. As a bit of fun Jack related how Harry had been insulted by the bar tender for being so long-winded in ordering the drinks. Jack knew that it was a sore point with Harry, but what was the harm – Harry didn't even know about the book?

In reviewing his manuscript a few months later Jack decided to remove the reference about the bar tender. He was glad he did, because Harry later heard about the book via Vera and asked to read it.

Being diplomatic

A comment that sounded funny when first written might not appear quite as amusing once reviewed at a later date. For the sake of diplomacy, take this opportunity to to revise your writing. Once down in print, it's there for ever!

Finalising the title

If you have not settled on a title, the time is looming when you will have to make a decision. Hopefully, by now you will have a shortlist of ideas. Bouncing these around with a close friend may help to arrive at the final choice.

Revising the grammar

It is amazing how many simple mistakes can be found when reading through an entire manuscript, but take comfort from the fact that the more you spot the less are left for your readers to tease you about.

Remember to pay particular attention to names, especially family names, as well as dates of birth, etc.

Referring to your house style

Before you start reading through the manuscript review what you wrote for your house style. You might want to refine this, but once you settle on a style use that throughout the manuscript. Consistency in simple matters, like double or single quotation marks, will at least avoid frustrating the reader.

Looking for anything that jumps out

If words jump out at you they need changing. Similarly, if you stumble over a phase, simplify it. Your words should not draw the attention of the reader away from the story.

Avoiding too many helpful, interesting, clever adjectives

We can sometimes try too hard to be descriptive – perhaps a throwback to English lessons at school when the teacher wanted to assess the diversity of our vocabulary. There is no such test here; too many adjectives can be annoying and the implication is that you are trying too hard. A well-chosen adjective is far more powerful than three or four bland ones.

Dealing with repetition

Sometimes repetition is used to provide emphasis: 'The house was huge, the garden was huge, the swimming pool was huge.' Unless you have deliberately sought to employ this technique, try using a different word.

Identifying favourite word syndrome

We all have favourite words which we overuse. If these jump out at you reduce their frequency. An independent proof-reader will help you identify these, and the word search facility on a word processor can also be helpful.

Clarifying ambiguities

If something sounds ambiguous to you, it is almost certain that the reader will be in the dark. Be particularly wary when using 'he' or 'she' when there are several people mentioned – don't forget, you know the story, your reader does not.

Seeking assistance

A fresh pair of eyes is always useful in proofreading – knowing what comes next makes it all too easy to miss our own mistakes.

Finding an independent proofreader

A friend or relative might be very happy to read your manuscript. If so, make it clear that you are looking for an objective review and that you will not be offended if they come back with dozens, or even hundreds, of queries. Friends can sometimes shy away from a vigorous review in an attempt not to offend.

To avoid any awkwardness, you might prefer to employ a professional proofreader – it is not as expensive a service as you might imagine. Sources can be found at the end of this book.

Independent proofreaders have the advantage over a friend or relative in that they do not know you and therefore cannot make certain assumptions. If they don't know who Fred is, they will say so. They are therefore more likely to pick up on any continuity and structural inconsistencies.

Opting for a collaborative review

If you are having your manuscript proofread, consider reviewing the manuscript together. Two minds are certainly better than one when it comes to revising a manuscript – the exercise is more thorough and great fun.

Reading aloud

If your assistant reads aloud you will hear your book as others will read it. In listening to the emphasis placed on the narrative, any clumsiness or ambiguity will jump out at you, resulting in the need to either rephrase a few words or alter the punctuation.

If you do opt for the collaborative approach, ensure that you can sit down together for a few hours at a time where you will not be disturbed. Also allow for the fact that your assistant is likely to ask questions about your story which will result in the need to elaborate on your writing in certain areas.

Association of Personal Historians (APH)

To quote from the APH website: "The Association of Personal Historians is a not-for-profit international trade association.

The purpose of the Association is to advance the profession of assisting individuals, organisations, and communities to preserve their histories, life stories and memories."

The APH lists over 500 organisations helping to preserve life stories in book form, orally or via DVD. Whilst most members operate from the US and Canada, there are members in the UK and Europe. These can be located under the 'Find a Personal Historian' icon on their excellent website www.personalhistorians.org

Making the word processor work for you

If you have used a typewriter, written in longhand or dictated your life story, it is likely that you will want it transcribed onto a word processor at some stage. This will give you greater choice for the production of your book, more of which will be discussed in the next chapter.

If you employ someone to do this for you, it is worth paying a little more for them to undertake some basic editing at the same time. However, ensure that you give clear guidelines as to how much initiative they can exercise – perhaps asking them to place a pencil mark along any passages they revise.

However good your typist/editor is, some alterations will be required when you review their work. In correcting your mistakes they are sure to introduce some of their own. Ensure that any alterations will be undertaken in a timely and cost-effective manner.

Using the spell check facility
The spell check facility is wonderful, but can lead to laziness when reviewing a manuscript. Most spell checks only pick out incorrectly spelt words, making it easy to overlook such common typing mistakes as 'our' instead of 'out'.

A book compiled from the diary of a dairy farmer produced some fun and games, with both words appearing many times! Where the obvious potential exists for mistakes like this, it is worth checking both words on the search facility.

Most word processors have a default setting of English (US). To avoid the appearance of Americanised words like favorite and organize, ensure that the spell check is altered to English (UK).

Using the grammar check facility

As mentioned earlier, over-dependence on the grammar check facility can diminish the character of a book. However, they are useful in checking the context of words. For example, it would highlight the 'our/out' problem defined above.

Attaining perfection

Unless you are a rare genius, forget the idea of perfection in a book of 50,000 or more words. Sadly, most books contain errors... maybe even this won. You can proofread your manuscript 83 times, and on the 84th reading still spot another mistake.

It is important to reduce the number of errors as much as possible, but family and friends love you for being you. If this is your audience, they won't mind if there is the odd glitch – it is inevitable.

Checklist

- Is the style of your first chapter consistent with subsequent chapters?
- Are you happy with your chapter headings?
- Have you written the sort of book you intended?

Assignments

    📖 Rewrite the introduction.

    📖 Revise any writing you feel uncomfortable about before it's too late.

    📖 Think of someone who can help you with proofreading and decide if you would like a collaborative approach.

Presentation 13

The purpose of this chapter is to provide options for the presentation of your book. First impressions are so important, and having worked hard on getting your manuscript right, it is worth spending time on the final presentation. Something well presented and pleasing to the eye will increase the reader's enjoyment immeasurably and also provide you with considerable satisfaction.

In this chapter we shall be looking at the presentation of a single book. Producing additional copies in a cost-effective manner, and the use of current technology, will be considered in the following chapters.

Choosing your medium

Many of the principles for presentation are the same whether the manuscript is handwritten, or produced on a typewriter or a word processor. A book can be achieved via any of these, although more advanced forms of presentation, like changing the size of the font, will require a word processor. Such options will be considered at length in Chapters 16 and 17.

Transcribing the manuscript

If you had intended to keep your manuscript in a handwritten format, but have revised that decision, it is worth considering having it typed onto a word processor. Not only will this help in terms of presentation and production, it allows changes to be made to your writing at any time. In addition to correcting inevitable mistakes, you can remove writing where you have had second thoughts, or insert more as you think of things you forgot to include.

It is relatively easy to have your manuscript transferred onto a word processor. Indeed, if it has been neatly typed on a typewriter, it should be possible to have it scanned, which will be cheaper still.

If the manuscript is to be word-processed:

- Agree a price by the number of words typed, not per hour. This ensures that the bill is not open to question and can be easily checked.
- Set parameters on what may be altered in your original manuscript. Spelling mistakes should be corrected as a matter of course, but most manuscripts also benefit from some 'gentle editing'. Satisfy yourself with the initiative of the person concerned and check if this alters the price.
- Obtain quotations from at least two or three different sources as prices can vary considerably.
- Agree in advance how changes will be made. These will probably have to be charged per hour.
- In addition to receiving the manuscript on paper, ensure that you are also provided with the files on disk. This way you have the option of going elsewhere for editing or further copies.

Suggestions for finding typing services can be found at the back of this book.

Refusing to be bullied

If the prospect of having to deal with technology more sophisticated than an electric kettle fills you with dread, don't be bullied into having to master a computer. Writing your life story in whatever format is a great achievement and should be celebrated.

You may be happy to accept the offer of a friend or someone in the family to transfer your writing onto a word processor, but establish the scope of the arrangement first. It can lead to complications on both sides – one party wondering when it is going to be finished and the other not appreciating quite how much is involved. Such complications are overcome by using independent help, but make sure you know what you are getting into.

Whatever your decision, don't let it ruin your enjoyment of having embarked on the project in the first place. However it is presented, your life story will be treasured by generations for years to come.

Conducting some simple research

Collect a dozen or more books from around your house and scrutinise them closely. Try to choose as many different styles as possible, including those containing pictures and other illustrations.

With a critical eye, now look at such attributes as:

- the size of the page
- the size and style of font
- spacing between lines
- margins
- the opening few pages
- the style of chapter headings and any other titles
- how pictures are presented and their associated captions
- any appendices.

Defining your own style

As a result of this research decide which presentations you like best and why. Don't limit your expectations – with modern production techniques plenty of options are available to you. For example, pictures do not have to appear in one block in the middle of the book but can be inserted at the appropriate place in the story.

It is often easier to spot what you do not like about the presentation of a particular book. Maybe the size of the writing is too small making it hard to read, or the pages come across as being heavy on the eye because of small margins.

Deciding on the size of the book

Q: What book dimensions do you recommend?

A: The dimensions of the book depend on how much has been written and the number of copies required. If you are looking for a handful of leather-bound presentation volumes, it is worth considering something approaching A4 size (the standard paper size in the UK). The larger page means that more pictures can be included to best effect… and more pictures to a page helps keep costs down.

Such a volume can easily contain upwards of 100,000 words. At the lower end, at least 25,000 words are recommended unless a large number of photos are to be included. Where there are fewer words, or a more modest book size is required, the pages can be guillotined to smaller dimensions.

For those using technology to produce larger print runs, book size will be considered further in Chapter 17.

Preparing the prelims

The 'prelims' are the preliminaries – everything that goes into the book before you get to the story itself. In the books you research, there will be a combination of most or all of the following:

- title page
- publisher details
- frontispiece photo
- dedication
- acknowledgements
- foreword
- contents
- illustration index
- preface or introduction
- prologue.

Strangely enough, the prelims also cover the pages at the back of the book, but we will come to these later.

Even more confusing is the fact that some of the above terms are used interchangeably and not in any strict order. The biggest offender is the 'introduction'. Usually this is written by the author to explain what has been done and why – a roadmap to the book. In this sense, it is another word for preface. However, it is sometimes used instead of or alongside the prologue or, more commonly, the foreword. On the assumption that 'anything goes', choose what you want… after all, it's *your* book!

Convention dictates that the first paper page is page 3 (as the front of the book is strictly page 1), and the early prelims (such as title page, photo etc) are not printed with the number showing, although they are counted in the run of the book.

Title page
This is simple enough. It merely states the title of the book, and perhaps a subtitle, along with your name. The important

thing here is to ensure that the page is well presented as it is what the reader sees first in your book.

How your name appears is entirely up to you, and is dependent upon the audience for your book. Below are a few suggestions:

- Dr W.L. Barton MBE, FRCPE
- Dr William Barton MBE
- Dr Bill Barton
- Bill Barton
- Grandpa

Publisher details
This includes by whom, when and where the book was published or produced. For private productions this is not strictly necessary, especially as anyone who helped you is likely to be mentioned in the acknowledgements.

This page also includes the copyright details. Anything you write of an original nature becomes your copyright as soon as the ink hits the page. The same is also true of material produced on a word processor or dictated onto tape. There is not even any need to write 'Copyright Michael Oke 2006' … but it is rather satisfying to see it in print so you may as well indulge yourself after all your hard work!

Frontispiece photo
While you probably did not see this in any of the books you researched, a picture of the author is a pleasing touch at the front of a life story. A photo in your earlier years, maybe between 15 and 25, is even better, because you can end the book with an up-to-date picture to provide symmetry.

A picture at the beginning is best placed after the title page or the dedication.

Dedication
Books don't have to have a dedication, but it seems a shame to miss the opportunity, and inclusion will always be very special to those mentioned.

You might want to dedicate the book to the memory of a loved one, and/or opt for a catchall:

> 'This book is dedicated to my entire family, past, present and future, and especially to my wife Mychelle whose love and support is treasured.'

Acknowledgements
This section is used to give thanks to all those who have assisted in the writing of the book. If your son painstakingly typed your manuscript into the small hours of the morning on many occasions, it is at least worth thanking him. Similarly, an unpaid friend may have spent dozens of hours proofreading the manuscript … even though you might not have agreed with all the comments.

It is also worth thanking your partner for allowing you the space to write the book, for providing countless cups of tea, answering your telephone calls and giving encouragement when it was needed.

Some people also like to include, '… and to my parents, without whom none of this would have been possible.' You might not want to go this far, but you get the idea.

Foreword
The purpose of this section is to commend the book to the reader; it is therefore usually written by someone other than the author. For commercial books, the publisher likes to see a well-known name on the cover to help increase sales.

Most private books do not have a foreword, but there is nothing to stop you doing so if you have someone special in mind.

Contents

The table of contents simply and clearly lists the chapters and any other sections, such as an index or any appendices. The convention is to begin listing the sections from this page onwards.

Illustrations index

This is not compulsory, but if you have included pictures it's a good idea to provide a listing... if only to make it easier for the family to find pictures of themselves.

Preface or introduction

In an autobiography this section usually explains why you embarked on the project and for whom the book was written. You will have drafted most of this at the outset of the project, revising it towards the end. It should therefore be in pretty good shape by this time and will only require a few adjustments.

Something else for you to consider including in this section is a sentence to protect you against the grumblings of any pedantic readers:

> 'This book was written with the best of intentions, so please forgive any offence caused by what I have either included or omitted... certainly none is intended.'

Prologue

This is strictly the start of the book, but is slightly separate from the main story.

Considering the prelims at the end of the book!

There are fewer sections to consider at the end of the book, although not necessarily fewer pages if there are extensive appendices:

- afterword or epilogue
- appendices
- index
- bibliography.

Afterword or epilogue

This tends to be included where something significant has happened since the conclusion of the writing. It may be that the life story was only written up until the Millennium, or perhaps the scope of the book was to cover a career or until the children left home. In such cases, a brief update can be provided regarding what happened in the intervening years. A subsequent edition or reprint of the book may be subject to similar treatment.

Considering an appendix

An appendix can include anything which does not fit neatly into your story:

- diaries you kept in early life
- the diary or writing of a parent or grandparent
- report cards throughout your school years
- census returns
- a family tree
- a list of important family dates
- songs or poetry
- sketches you performed
- a soapbox
- a log of your round the world cruise.

If you get carried away and the appendix starts to form a life of its own, it might be better to think again. You could perhaps place these materials in a special box in which you keep your book. This will ensure that the appendix does not detract from the intended focus of the book – your life story.

Including reminiscences from the wider family

If you have asked your children, or perhaps a sibling, cousin or friend, to write a few pages, it is likely to fit comfortably as an appendix.

An account written by your partner can be included as an appendix, but it is usually best found within the main body of the book.

Producing a family tree

A family tree that fits onto a single page of your book can be readily accommodated as an appendix. However, family trees have a tendency to extend with the enthusiasm of research. If it cannot be produced on a single page, or perhaps folded into a reasonable size to be slotted into the back of the book, it might be best not to include it.

An advantage of keeping the family tree separate is that it can be updated as the need arises and new copies can replace those that become dog-eared and torn with regular unfolding. It can perhaps be kept in the presentation box along with the book.

Further advice on how to deal with family trees can be found in Chapter 17.

Index

The complexities involved in compiling an index tend to make them unrealistic unless a word processor is used. This subject is therefore considered in Chapter 17.

Bibliography

Whilst a bibliography is more commonly found in academic books, there is no reason why you should not include one if you have used quotations in your book, possibly in conjunction with chapter headings.

Designing the book

However you choose to produce your book, an appreciation of what is possible will provide better results. Using quality paper, inserting photographs and investing in an impressive binding will transform a photocopied handwritten text. Additionally, for those seeking help to produce their books, it is worth knowing what to look out for. This section on design provides an overview of what should be considered. For those intending to design their own book on a word processor, technical information can be found in Chapter 17.

The measure of a well-presented book is how pleasing it is to the eye. However, as is often the case, creating something simple involves some complex considerations.

Creating the first impression

Our first impressions of a page are dictated by:

- the style of the font
- the size of the font
- the size of the margins
- the layout
- the quality of print.

Choosing the font

If your book is handwritten, the style and size of your writing will have been honed over many years. Your greatest consideration will be legibility – if your handwriting is poor, you must consider having the manuscript typed.

The more sophisticated typewriters, and all modern word processors and printers, will give you a selection of font styles and sizes. Experiment to see what looks best, perhaps also asking a few friends for their opinions.

Adjusting the margins

Small margins make the page look overloaded with text. Increasing the size of the margins can have a dramatic effect on the appearance. Again, it is worth experimenting.

If the book is to be bound, the edges will need to be guillotined. You will need to leave larger margins to allow for this. While margins are still of consideration with the handwritten text, if lined paper is being used, the top, bottom and left-hand margins will be pre-set. Of greater importance here is the space between the lines. Again, experiment until you feel comfortable with the overall appearance.

Designing the page layout

Too many words on a page can leave the reader feeling daunted – plenty of space will improve the appearance of your book significantly. However, there are a few other considerations worth bearing in mind.

Dealing with speech

If you have decided to use speech within the book, this can be presented two ways:

- Within the run of the text:
  When Mary came into the room she exclaimed, 'Boys, what on earth do you think you're doing?' Ted, taken totally by surprise, stuttered, 'We we we we're, ju-just looking for my old photo album ...'
- As scripted conversation:
  – 'What's for tea, Mum?' asked Jim.
  – 'Sausages,' came back the reply.
  – 'Great. Can Billy stay for tea? His mum says it's OK.'
  – 'Thanks for asking me first,' Mum quipped.

The decision rests with you, but where there are more than two or three exchanges, scripting the conversation is worth considering.

Presenting paragraphs

Again, there are two conventions to consider:

- indenting the first word of a new paragraph
- leaving a line between paragraphs, starting new ones on the left margin.

Either is fine, as long as you are consistent within the book.

Handling headings

Be careful to ensure that each chapter heading appears with the same spacing and font size and type.

Using section breaks

Sometimes within a chapter there is a change of subject. The use of a few asterisks will show the reader that you are moving on to a new section.

* * * * *

Selecting pictures

Pictures will significantly enhance the overall appearance of your book. You might like to consider such things as:

- photographs
- certificates
- ration book
- identity card
- sketches
- documents
- school reports
- cartoons
- special cards
- newspaper cuttings.

Achieving the right balance

The majority of pictures are likely to be photographs of family and people who have been significant in your life. Especially with pictures of the family, it is important to ensure a balance. If there are six photos of your daughter and only two of your son, he might feel offended. Counting the number of times that people appear in the book can be revealing.

While you may be besotted with any grandchildren or god-children, it must be remembered that this is a book about your whole life. The early photographs are usually far more fascinating than those taken relatively recently.

Q: How many photographs should I include?

A: There are no hard and fast rules. Some people have half a dozen pages of pictures, others include 50 or more … and four or five pictures can fit on a page. However, the more pages of pictures you include, the greater the reproduction costs.

Photographs are interesting, especially those in your early life, but selecting them is not easy. Ultimately, you can include as many as you like, but remember that this is an autobiography and not a photograph album. The photos should not detract from the writing – they are there to enhance it.

Selecting the right place for the pictures

Placing pictures in a handwritten or typed presentation requires a great deal of forethought and it will be easier to resort to the traditional-style block of pictures, or a page of pictures inserted nearest to the appropriate point.

With a word processor there is far more flexibility and pictures can be placed at the appropriate point in the text.

Adding captions

Captions in a book serve a similar purpose to writing on the backs of photos. While we know who everyone is at the time, with the passing of years it becomes increasingly difficult to identify everyone. Even if the book is aimed at a purely family audience, unless the picture is placed immediately next to the relevant text, it is worth adding captions.

Ensure that the captions are also proofread – any mistakes are likely to be immediately spotted because the pictures will be looked at more often than the text. Additionally, as the manuscript is usually proofread before the pictures are inserted, captions can escape being proofed.

Choosing the final picture

The last picture in the book occupies a very significant position. A photograph of yourself in later life is fitting; other favourites are a picture of the whole family, or perhaps one of you and your partner if that is appropriate.

This picture should normally appear on the final page of the book, just before any appendix.

Reproducing the pictures

Even for a single book it is unlikely that you will want to use the original photographs or other templates. However, various forms of high quality reproductions can be found at surprisingly affordable prices:

- copy photographs
- photocopying (black and white and colour)
- computer scanning.

Ordering copy photographs

Where you have photographs, copies can be easily ordered from high street or mail order outlets. For other templates take a photograph and then order as many copies as you require.

The pictures can be inserted into the appropriate space left in the text using double-sided tape.

The disadvantage of this process is that the final book will be a little bulky because the photos stand proud of the page.

Using photocopies

While regular black and white copies may be adequate, the quality of colour photocopies is excellent, often being hard to distinguish from the original photograph or document. Copy shops can be found in most high streets.

Photocopying pictures

Pictures up to A4 or even A3 size can be accommodated, being reduced as necessary to fit the size of your book.

If individual copy pictures are to be stuck onto the pages of your manuscript, better value can be obtained by placing several photographs on one page, having them photocopied and then cutting them up.

Once cut to size, the pictures can be inserted with adhesive or double-sided tape at the appropriate place in the text. As photocopies are thinner than photographs, the book will be less bulky than using copy photos.

Photocopying the whole page

An alternative method is to place the photograph within the text and then photocopy the whole page. This can lead to varying results because text and photographs do not always reproduce to the same quality. However, with perseverance, excellent results can be obtained and, of course, the picture remains flush with the page.

A word of warning – if your requirements are too complex or demanding, you may be charged for trial copies as well as the final versions.

Scanning the pictures

Computer technology is such that pictures can be scanned and reproduced in colour to a very high definition; again, it is often difficult to distinguish the reproduction from the original.

Because of the almost limitless flexibility of technology and high quality printers, excellent results can be obtained. The pictures and the text can be manipulated at will, but because of the time-consuming nature of the process, it can be expensive, unless you do it yourself.

Selecting the paper

Here you face an amazing array of choice. Any high street stationer will have access to hundreds of types and qualities of paper with different weights, grains, colours, tints, etc.

For a good-looking result, try something a little heavier than the standard 80 gsm, perhaps 90 or 100. Shiny papers are perhaps a little too bright, whereas antique papers can be too dull – for some. Again, it is a matter of personal taste.

One tip – many stationers sell papers specially designed for this or that printer, with this or that purpose in mind. While it is true that some papers won't work well in certain machines, most of this is an excuse to sell paper at inflated prices. Glossy paper doesn't always work well in inkjet printers, and laser printers become incredibly hot. Also, most domestic printers struggle to print on anything much thicker than 120 gsm. All the other considerations are aimed at office and professional users, so don't be bamboozled by a very confusing market.

If you have environmental concerns, there are also plenty of papers that come from sustainable sources, which are now not much more expensive than normal papers. These also normally work fine in domestic printers.

Paper is incredibly cheap, so shop around, ask for samples, and when you are happy that what you like will work in your printer, stick with it.

Reproducing the text

If your manuscript is handwritten, or typed on a typewriter with no memory, and you only want one copy of the book you can use your original script. However, if, as is likely, several books are required, the manuscript will need to be photocopied.

For those using a word processor and printer, or an electronic typewriter with a memory, this is not an issue as additional copies can be reproduced at the touch of a button.

Pictures scanned into the computer can be printed along with text. If the pictures are to be attached afterwards, an appropriate space will need to be left within the printed page.

Demanding high quality

A good printer is vital for a quality production. Inkjet and laser printers are amazingly cheap; alternatively, you may be able to borrow one from a friend or relative.

Other issues to consider are:

- good quality paper (at least 80 gsm)
- using a new toner cartridge
- leaving plenty of space for pictures.

Checklist

- ꙮ Have you included everyone who has helped you with the book in the acknowledgements?
- ꙮ Are you happy with the balance of pictures?
- ꙮ Have you checked for consistency in the text, and the layout of the pages and headings?

Assignments

- ꙮ Decide on the size of the book and how it is to be presented: handwritten, typed or word processed.
- ꙮ Finalise the introductory pages.
- ꙮ Investigate how you would like to reproduce the pictures.
- ꙮ Produce the final draft of the book.

Production

14

This chapter looks at simple ways to produce a modest number of books for family and friends. Those looking for print on demand and/or self-publishing to produce larger numbers of books will find further help in the final chapters.

Q: What is print on demand?

A: Digital technology has brought a revolution to the print industry. Without the need for expensive plates and litho systems, it is now possible to send a CD (or even transmit the data over the internet) to have individual high quality books produced. Whilst in theory you can order one book, due to some small overheads it is more cost-effective to think in terms of ordering ten or twenty books at a time. It is important that the information is received in precisely the correct format, as any help required, or changes made to your files, will be charged at premium rates.

Producing a single volume

Now that you have the final manuscript of your book, possibly also including pictures, you are in a position to have it transformed into a book.

Whether your manuscript is handwritten, typed or word processed, you have several options available to you.

Having your manuscript bound

Witnessing a pile of paper being transformed into a book is an amazing experience. In the hands of an expert bookbinder, the manuscript is stitched and bound, providing a beautiful and fitting presentation for all your hard work.

Most universities will be happy to recommend the bookbinder they use for PhD theses; alternatively, the telephone directory may list a local firm. Depending on what material is used (leather, buckram, etc.), it is likely to cost in the region of £20 to £30 per copy.

Q: I want to have my book bound – how many pages does it need to be?

A: For a book to be bound you should have at least 75 sheets – 150 sides. Up to 500 sides can be accommodated comfortably before considering dividing your work into a second volume.

If you need to increase the number of pages you have several options:

– write more
– include more pictures
– consider an appendix or two
– encourage other contributions.

With the use of a word processor you can also:

- opt for a book with smaller dimensions
- increase the margins
- increase the font size.

It is likely that you will choose several of the above and play around with different page layouts before you arrive at the presentation that is most pleasing to the eye.

Incorporating larger pictures
With careful folding it should be possible to include the occasional large picture or, more likely, a family tree. The bookbinder is likely to guillotine the edge of the book, so discuss how any special pages should be folded.

If this service cannot be offered, the bookbinder may be willing to add a small pocket in the back or front inside cover in which to hold a folded sheet of paper.

Considering other forms of presentation
More modest productions will include:

- a ring binder
- a photograph album
- spiral binding (plastic or wire)
- heat-treated glue bindings
- metal clamp bindings.

One of your simplest options is to produce your book on A4 pages, and then keep it in a smart ring binder, or take it to the local copy shop and have it comb-bound. Inexpensive and effective, it will preserve the document and you can easily change and add to it later.

For a more long-lasting finish, contact a few local printers, copy shops and binders to see what options they offer. Printers may be able to produce stapled booklets (for smaller documents), or perfect-bound paperbacks (where the sheets are glued into a cover to form a traditional paperback book). Additionally, large office superstores have an abundance of presentation ideas that are worth investigating.

Producing a cover

Despite the saying, 'Never judge a book by its cover' – we do!

Whether you use a ring binder, or produce a paperback or hardback, a cover will give the book even greater impact. The possibilities here are endless, but again, the advice is to keep it simple. Unless you had a career as an illustrator, people want to read about you, not be impressed by your artistic skills. Perhaps you know someone who has some design ability – ask them to help. A ring binder can be covered with a simple sheet including the title and a photograph from your life reproduced on it.

Paperbacks or hardbacks demand something more. If computer software scares you, then ask the binder/printer to help you. The technicalities of designing and printing a cover the right size are quite complicated, but you can always ask the professionals to include a picture, a selection of pictures, or a design of your choice.

If you do fancy designing your own cover, advice can be found in Chapter 17.

Producing multiple copies

Photocopying
Photocopying can be a cost-effective way of producing a small number of books, especially if you do not have your own computer system. For example, if a friend has helped you to produce a high quality single manuscript, there is nothing to

stop you having it photocopied and bound into a modest number of books.

Colour photocopies are excellent quality, and by shopping around you should receive some attractive prices. You will have to ensure that the pages are collated properly before having them bound, but for a small number of copies that is not an onerous job.

Printing through the photocopier

Many copy shops can provide a service of printing your book through the photocopier. You provide the digital file, either on CD or downloaded to their email address, and they produce your manuscript perfectly printed as many times as you require. This may be a particularly attractive option if your own printer is not of the highest quality, like an inkjet printer. Should more copies be required at a later date, they can be provided just as effortlessly.

It could be educational to pop along to the copy shop for a chat, not least because toner for domestic printers is not cheap and the cost of producing your own copies can soon escalate.

Printing your own copies

Many people find this option attractive, not least because there is something very satisfying about seeing your own book coming off the printer. As mentioned above, the price of toner cartridges can add up, so it is worth keeping on top of costs.

Having gone to all the effort of writing your life story, it is worth ensuring a decent print quality for your book. Inkjet printers are adequate, but you will probably appreciate the better quality of a laser printer. They are remarkably afford-able, but if you don't want to invest in one for a few books, consider using the copy shop as discussed above, or perhaps a print on demand service.

Considering print on demand

If you require dozens of copies of your book, or if you simply relish the technical challenge, print on demand services can be very cost-effective. While in principle it is possible to order single copies, by the time you have paid set-up costs and included packing and postage it is more realistic to think in terms of ordering at least ten or twenty books. As this is unlikely to be a problem, this is an option well worth considering.

Print on demand and self-publishing will be considered in detail in Chapters 16 and 17.

Celebrating your book

If you are not looking to pursue more technological options, you might like to look at some final snippets of advice provided in Chapter 18. Apart from that, you have finished – well done!

Whether you have produced one book or several, you have achieved a major feat. So many people say, 'I could write a book,' but very few do so.

Savour the moment and perhaps throw a party for your book launch. If it has been written in secret, you can plan the surprise unveiling of your book. You might even want to invite the local press.

Failing that, why not go out for a special dinner to mark the occasion – after all, it's not every day that you write a book. Don't forget to include those who've helped; they will want to share your special day.

Again, well done.

What next?

With all the time you will find that you now have on your hands, there are any number of possibilities open to you. Perhaps you can consider:

- reading your book onto a tape recorder or digital camera
- joining a writing circle
- setting up a life writing class
- writing articles for magazines
- researching your family tree
- helping others with their books
- writing a sequel!

Checklist

- Are you happy with the binding? Having come this far you don't want to spoil the overall presentation for the sake of a few pounds.
- Are you sure about how many copies of the book you require?

Assignments

- Plan your book launch.
- Relax and enjoy the party.

Publishing

15

Publishing is a complex industry and while it is not the main intention of this book to encourage authors in this direction, some ideas and warnings are provided for the more adventurous. Those who wish to pursue self-publishing will find help in the remaining chapters.

Considering publishing

Various forms of publishing exist, and not all are what they claim to be. Many people have paid significant sums of money for little in return, so tread very carefully. Vanity publishers like to refer to their services as 'self-publishing', so read this whole section carefully.

For ease of discussion, publishing shall be considered under three broad categories:

              ❧   mainstream publishing
              ❧   vanity publishing
              ❧   self-publishing.

Understanding mainstream publishing

Writing that bestseller

We have all heard of the unknown author writing a bestseller ... we rarely hear of the tens of thousands who remain unknown.

If you suspect that your manuscript may appeal to a wider audience you might be tempted to look for a publisher.

Identifying mainstream publishers

Mainstream publishers do not expect any payment; they receive their return from a percentage of the sale of the books. Indeed, some publishers even give an advance, but to receive one you are likely to be a nationally known figure, or at least have a track record as an author.

Being realistic, you will not receive an advance, and are extremely unlikely to have your manuscript accepted by a reputable publisher.

Slogging around

Hundreds of publishers and the types of books in which they specialise are listed in *The Writers' and Artists' Yearbook* and *The Writers' Handbook*. Many will not accept unsolicited manuscripts, but others are happy to do so. Research well, be patient and do not raise your hopes.

Publishers usually require a synopsis of the book and a sample chapter. By enclosing a stamped addressed envelope your manuscript should be returned to you.

Finding an agent

You may be very lucky and find an agent who will hawk your manuscript round publishing houses on your behalf. However, finding an agent is likely to be equally as difficult as approaching the publisher in the first place.

Agents are also listed in *The Writers' and Artists' Yearbook* and *The Writers' Handbook*.

Warning

If you have seen an advert offering to publish your book, in all likelihood this will not be a mainstream publisher as they rarely advertise – they don't need to as they are hounded by dozens of would-be authors every day.

Understanding vanity publishing

Vanity publishers feast upon the unrealistic optimism of new authors. Understandably, they never advertise their services as vanity publishers, being more likely to call themselves 'cooperative publishers', 'subsidy publishers' or even using the generic title of self-publishing.

Vanity publishers imply that huge quantities of your book will be sold, although they are careful not to state this in writing. Rarely do they sell more than one or two copies – that is essentially left to you. No company can guarantee large sales … and if they could, they should be offering you an advance in the first place.

Furthermore, you often do not even receive the books until you make sales, in the process sending even more money on top of the substantial prepayment!

If you spend money, at least get books in return and be prepared to sell them yourself.

Considering self-publishing

A more realistic outlet for the unknown autobiographer is via self-publishing. Here the author arranges for a number of books to be printed, registers the ISBN and then undertakes any promotion of the books. Essentially, the author also becomes the publisher.

Some authors are happy with a limited number of copies to give or sell to a largely known audience, perhaps with the option of ordering more copies if demand goes well. Others relish a greater challenge and want to try their chances in appealing to a wider audience.

Understanding the risks

Self-publishing involves the author taking the risk of production in the hope of recouping those costs and, hopefully, more when and if the book is sold. The onus remains with the author to sell the books. This is fine as long as you go in with your eyes open and are prepared to accept the risks.

Books were traditionally ordered from a printer, but with the advance of technology, print on demand offers an increasingly attractive option to the author.

Looking for a local printer

If you require at least 250 copies of your book it is worth obtaining a quotation from your local printer. You will be advised as to what is involved and be provided with a fixed price for the books. Armed with this information you can investigate what sort of market there might be for your book.

The price of books from a printer becomes increasingly attractive the more you order. However, don't be tempted to order thousands when you know that you only have requests for 53 copies … you may end up with an awful lot of books under your bed.

Considering print on demand

Books generated by computer incur fewer overheads than a printing press. Set-up costs are lower and so competitive prices can be offered for a modest number of books. These can be ordered in units of ten to twenty at a time, rather than hundreds as with conventional printing. If the author waits for confirmed orders before requesting a batch of books, the risk is reduced solely to the original set-up cost.

Taking precautions

If you are looking to produce your books via a third party:

- Ensure that you have a written quotation of all costs before embarking on any venture.
- Ask to see samples of the type of book you will receive.
- Speak to previous customers.
- Ensure that you will receive a proof before the books are printed, and check this proof thoroughly – it is your responsibility.

With the options considered so far you will know how much the books cost in advance. Whoever undertakes the book production makes no guarantees as to how many may be sold – that is entirely up to you.

Beware of anyone who makes claims about how many books you will sell, especially if you are paying for the privilege.

Obtaining an ISBN

Published books require an International Standard Book Number, a unique number that will allow your book to be ordered from anywhere in the world. Details can be found at the back of this book under Useful Addresses.

While the service is free, you will be required to provide six copies of your book for depositing in various libraries. It also entitles you to an entry in the magazine *Bookseller*, which is received by bookshops.

You will need to nominate a publisher. This is likely to be yourself and you will then be contacted by any bookshop that receives an order for your book. Again, don't raise your hopes; unless your book receives tremendous publicity, you are unlikely to receive many (if any) orders.

Promoting your book

Those who receive a precious copy of your book are likely to be delighted – after all, it has been lovingly written by their friend. Don't be tempted into thinking that such praise means that the book is destined to become a bestseller.

Testing the market

The real measure as to the commercial success of your book is whether people who do not know you are prepared to pay for it. To test this it is worth seeking independent advice, but this should not be sought from anyone who will ultimately charge you money – they are likely to say what you want to hear!

Approaching local bookshops

Local bookshops will be a potential outlet, but valuable shelf space will not be offered unless it is felt that your book will sell.

Before having any books printed, seek the opinion of the managers of these shops, asking such questions as:

- Would there be any demand for such a book?
- If so, in what numbers?
- What should the price of the book be?
- What percentage would the bookshop charge?
- Can you show me any similar books?
- How many copies were sold?

Bookshop managers will also give advice on printers of similar books, and probably also provide contact details of local people who have undertaken similar ventures. It is well worth approaching other such authors for their advice and warnings.

Having the book reviewed

The local newspaper will probably be happy to review your original book. You could mention that you are considering having the book printed and that anyone interested in a copy should contact you. The response you receive will help determine whether to proceed with a wider publishing venture.

Most people interested in buying a copy will be happy to wait a few months while books are being printed.

If your story includes a particular subject, like your time in the RAF, a specialist magazine or service association may be happy to review it.

Placing articles

If a magazine is happy to print a few pages of your book in the form of an article, this will help you gauge its wider appeal. If you are fortunate, you may even be able to persuade the magazine to pay you a few pounds for your efforts.

Asking friends

While friends are likely to speak favourably about your book, if you have wider aspirations it will be worth asking them whether they know of people who would be happy to buy a copy. If the result is a diplomatic, 'They can borrow mine,' then perhaps the market will not be quite as buoyant as you had hoped.

This may sound harsh, but it's better to be disappointed early on rather than to build your hopes, pay out good money and then be disappointed.

Making it work

While the advice here has been to err on the side of caution, some people make a success of self-publishing and have a hugely enjoyable time in the process. Success is usually measured by covering costs rather than making money, but they have the satisfaction of knowing that their book has been read by a wider audience than would otherwise be the case.

Checklist

- Are you sure you want to embark on publishing?
- If you have been asked to pay, are you comfortable with what is being offered? Have you seen samples of the work you are expecting and spoken to past clients?

Assignment

- If you are considering publishing, write a list of people who have confirmed that they would like to buy a copy.

Producing Your Own Book 16

Part 1 – General Considerations

Exploiting advances in technology

The rapid advance of technology over the last five to ten years has meant that it has become commonplace for anyone with a basic computer and a printer to produce their own documents. Word processing, desktop design and photographic software are relatively cheap (if not free), and computers have fallen in price so much that many homes now have them.

The advantage in this growth of technology is that now anyone can potentially write, design and print their own life story. Whilst very few people will ever enter the bestseller lists, books that you produce yourself can be just as satisfying, if not more so.

The last three chapters have looked at the presentation and production of different styles of books. This chapter outlines some of the basic issues that deal with turning your finished manuscript into a physical object which your friends and family can read. Whilst some of the material is similar, it is looked at from a technical perspective and includes options for use in Microsoft Word™. It assumes some computer knowledge, but does not expect you to be a technical guru.

If you don't have the desire to turn your manuscript into a book yourself, the routes already considered are obviously still open to you. Whether it is photocopying your typed pages and putting them into a ring binder, or taking your manuscript to a professional book producer, friends and family will be equally delighted that you have written your story.

Scoffing at the doom merchants

With the spread of computers and digital information, in the late 1990s the prophets of doom were foretelling the end of the book. Libraries would simply become large electronic databases, commuters and students would no longer read from paper but from portable ebook machines, and bookshops would close down and simply sell titles over the Internet.

However, the irony is that, whilst sales of ebooks and similar products have grown, the actual sales of physical books grow year on year. Publishers are putting out more titles, the number of publishing houses increases, and the media have begun to catch on – programmes on television and radio now encourage reading, support book groups and boost book sales enormously. In the midst of this phenomenal growth, more and more ordinary people are turning their manuscript into a finished book.

Checking the equipment

If you want to design and produce your own book, especially if you intend to scan and manipulate photographs, it is essential that you have a system which is both up-to-date and up to the task.

Software

Word processing

Microsoft™ is not only the dominant force in computer operating systems, with its Windows software, it also has established itself with the leading word processing program, Microsoft Word. While there are still other products and systems which are widely used (WordPerfect™ and Apple Mac™, for example), this chapter will look at book production through the eyes of someone using Word – for the simple reason that it is pretty much ubiquitous, and most people are therefore likely to have access to it if they are intending to produce their own book.

Word is updated roughly every year, and of course the latest versions have more bells and whistles than the previous incarnations. But beware, the more fancy things a program can do, the more likely it is that it will trip you up. Latest is not necessarily best. If you are not that advanced in using computer software, don't worry about having the most up-to-date package. Word 97™ onwards is sufficient for all simple book layout and design.

Desktop technology

Within the publishing world, most firms use bespoke software to design and produce books – programs such as Quark™ and Adobe PageMaker™. While these are fantastic and can produce remarkable results, they are designed for the professionals... and they come with a matching price tag! So, while any designer reading this may scoff at the use of a word processor for this task, Word is more than able to do the job. The demarcation line between word processing programs and desktop design is becoming more and more blurred anyway. If you are writing and producing your own life story, there is nothing to be gained from spending thousands on software.

Similarly, design programs can achieve fantastic results with pictures and images. However, if you decide that your manuscript is going to include a few pictures, again word processing programs can handle graphics sufficiently well for our purposes. Scanners (see below under 'hardware') are more often than not sold with image processing software which will convert the pictures into usable data; so again, don't be tempted to buy anything fancy.

Remember, this is a story about you and your life, not an attempt to show off your skills (or otherwise) at using a computer.

Hardware

Computer

Any computer purchased in the last five years should easily handle the design and layout of a simple manuscript. Don't worry too much about bytes and RAM if you are looking to produce a simple book. Mobile phones now have more computing power in them than the machines I used to start my business over fifteen years ago... but we still managed to produce beautiful books!

However, if you wish to include pictures in your document, then the processing power and memory of your computer is important. Electronic pictures take up a large amount of space on a computer's hard drive storage, and because they are made up of so much information, the computer also needs a good-sized processing memory to handle this information. So the storage disk (usually measured these days in gigabytes), the RAM size and the speed of the processor are important. Similarly, when using a computer for graphical tasks, the power of the graphics card is also significant. Having said all that, any machine purchased since 2003 will easily do the job... and any salesman who tries to tell you otherwise is thinking about their commission!

Scanner

Of course, if you are including images in your document, you need some way of obtaining those images. Old photographs and templates can easily be scanned on a flatbed scanner. They usually come with free processing software which allows you to scan the photographs, so don't be tempted by any fancy editing programs. Hand-held scanners rarely produce the required results, whereas high-end scanners are only really necessary for business users.

Digital cameras can be used to take up-to-date family photographs, for example, and possibly for taking pictures of over-sized photographs and memorabilia such as paintings or medals. Again, digital cameras have come down enormously in price, so unless you have aspirations to be a David Bailey, don't be tempted to spend a fortune. Images from a digital camera can be fed direct into the computer.

Printers
Inkjet printers

As with all hardware, there is an enormous range of printers now available. Basic inkjet printers are sold at give-away prices (beware, the manufacturers make their money on the consumables, not on the printers themselves!). For printing drafts of your book to look at, edit and generally work with along the way, inkjet printers are more than sufficient.

If you are producing your own book without photographs, a budget inkjet printer will meet all your requirements. If you wish to include black and white or colour pictures, inkjet printers can also produce impressive results, although it probably is worth spending a little more on the printer if images are important to you.

Laser printers

The other route which is becoming more popular, again due to the drop in price, is provided by laser printers. Laser printers generally produce a much crisper result, and for a long-lasting and impressive finish are worth the investment. Colour laser printers are also available at a budget price (rather than the thousands they used to cost), so if you are looking for a very professional finish, they may be the best option. However, this investment is probably only worth it if you intend to use the printer for other projects in the future. And remember, as with the inkjet printers, the money for the manufacturer is made from the consumables, so you might want to ration the number of pages you print!

Printers: memory

One final consideration for printers is their memory size. If your manuscript is going to contain numerous images, the final document could be so large in terms of megabytes that it will overload the memory of the printer. There are a number of solutions to this problem – buy more memory for your printer (expensive option), print the book in small sections, such as chapters (cheap and practical option, but more time-consuming), or convert your document into a 'print-ready' file which uses much less memory. The most common way of doing the last option is to prepare PDF files using Adobe Acrobat. PDFs have become standard throughout the printing world. They are easy to produce, but you do require the additional software and greater computer knowledge.

Using the professionals

Of course, you might like to design and prepare your book to the very last detail... and have someone else print it for you. Major towns and cities are littered with copy shops falling over themselves to take your business. They have already invested thousands of pounds in the latest printing machines, and will be more than willing to print your book for you. Most are familiar with doing so, but as in any market, the prices charged vary considerably.

Wider considerations

Once you have ensured you have the necessary equipment to undertake this project, some more research is required.

Being prepared

The copy shop will want to know what state the manuscript is in and the software you have used; they should ask lots of questions about what finished result you want. 'Is it print-ready?' will be a common question – basically this means, can the assistant just press a button and go?

Unfortunately, many amateurs think their project is print-ready, when in fact there are numerous details that have not been addressed. So beware of hidden charges from copy shops. Some such charges may be fully justifiable – for example, if the customer has neglected to set the page size of the document to match the final page size of the printer which the book will be printed on, the assistant will have to spend time adjusting the document accordingly. Or another example: the client submitting a manuscript where the sentences don't even have full stops or punctuation can hardly claim that the work is 'print-ready'.

Appreciating the costs

As with all skills, there are reasons why the professionals charge money for their services – they have been trained and are experienced in their profession. The advent of technology means that more and more people can have a go... but unfortunately it doesn't always mean that more and more people get it right! That's the whole purpose of this chapter – to help you get as much of your book ready as you feel able. If at any point you feel you can't take it any further, then there are plenty of people who can help you finish the task.

Designing your book

The issues on presentation discussed in Chapter 13 are the same however your book is produced. The benefit of using your own computer is that you can design precisely what you require and see the results before the book is produced. You will need to undertake the same research in deciding the type of book you want, but you can play around with page size, size and style of font, headings, paragraphs, line spacing, margins, etc to your heart's content.

Cost versus quality

The danger in looking at so many beautiful books and designing the perfect page is that it is easy to get carried away. The weight, quality and colour of paper all have price implications, as do the various styles of binding and cover. Then there is quality of photograph reproduction and whether you choose colour or black and white. Your budget may not extend to all your choices, but being well informed will give you a better chance of achieving your precise requirements.

Setting a budget

The reason why you are writing your life story will have implications for the type of book you end up with. If it is a labour of love for special friends and family, you may be prepared to pay accordingly. On the other hand, you might be hoping to cover costs, or even make money (possibly for charity). Either way, it can be helpful to decide on a budget in advance to prevent costs rising alarmingly.

Even using an external printing company, it is possible to produce books of a couple of hundred pages with black and white pictures for as little as £10 each on a print-run as small as 25. However, any additional help required, or an increase in the quality of the book, and prices can increase enormously.

A note of warning

Even if you are able to meet the exacting requirements of digital printing companies and achieve such modest prices, it will still be difficult to make money from your book. The marketing implications discussed in Chapter 15 hold true, and you will do well to cover costs.

Even if you are self-publishing, it is possible to slip into the realms of vanity publishing. You might not get your fingers burnt in the same way, but avoid over-ambitious expectations and keep the print-run to modest proportions. It is far more satisfying to order another 25 books than it is to look at the hundreds of spare copies lying around the house.

Checklist

- If you are intending to design your own book, ensure your software is compatible with current printers.
- If you want to scan pictures, check that you have sufficient RAM and memory on your computer.

Assignments

- ❦ Pop along to your local copy shop and ask what they require from you to print your book. Ensure that you see some samples of their work, looking closely at the quality of the print and the type of binding.
- ❦ Ask to speak to clients who have undertaken a similar venture – they are sure to have some invaluable advice and might even help you with your own project.
- ❦ Ask for a quotation for printing books in units of ten, 25, 50 and 100 and the associated reprint costs.

Microsoft, Word, Word 97 and Windows are registered trademarks of the Microsoft Corporation in the United States and/or other countries.

Apple and Mac are registered trademarks of the Apple Corporation in the United States and/or other countries.

WordPerfect is a registered trademark of The Corel Corporation, QuarkXPress is a registered trademark of Quark, and Pagemaker and Acrobat are registered trademarks of Adobe.

Producing Your Own Book
17

Part 2 – Technical Considerations

Making decisions

As too much choice can lead to complications, it is helpful to start making some decisions.

Selecting the size of the book

With modern software you can alter the page size at any time, but it is best to get this settled, as subsequent alterations will affect the placement of titles, pictures and chapter breaks. As with the other matters we will discuss, book size is mostly an issue of personal preference, although there are of course certain standard sizes that people have got used to because of their use in the book industry.

As A4 is the most common paper size in the UK, cost implications will dictate that you consider this as the maximum size of your book. A volume produced to the full size of A4 can look too much like a thesis or report, so unless you have strong preferences to the contrary, or a vast number of words to accommodate, it is worth considering something smaller.

A5 is half A4 and numerous books are produced in this size or smaller. However, if you want to include pictures, have reasonable margins and allow for the trimming required by those doing the binding, it is worth considering something between A4 and A5. As paper is relatively cheap, it is unlikely to be a significant factor in the price of the book, and a size larger than A5 can look more pleasing to the eye.

With Microsoft Word, you can set the size of your page to whatever you wish, specified in imperial or metric measurements. (Go to the Tools menu, choose Options, then click on the General tab. Towards the bottom of the box is a window to change the standard measurements used throughout Word.) The main factor limiting page size is, of course, the size of paper that a printer can accommodate. The majority of popular printers print on A4 and slightly larger sizes.

When deciding on your page size, it is best to think of some of the following factors:

- The number of words in the manuscript. Anything over 100,000 words starts to look bulky in a smaller book approaching A5 size. Anything under 25,000 words is a bit flimsy in an A4-size book.
- The size and style of font for the text and headings, and the spacing between lines. Each of these considerations will affect the size of the book (see below).
- The number of photographs (if any) to be included. One or two pictures can fit acceptably on a smallish page, but

of course beautiful pictures of high quality almost always look better when reproduced in a larger format. (Note: a picture scanned at low resolution will look grainy and blurred if enlarged excessively.)

📎 The amount of white space you find pleasing on a page. Larger margins can look impressive, set off the text to great effect and avoid a 'cluttered' appearance. (See under 'setting the margins' below.)

📎 The type of book you have written. If it is a book to curl up with in bed, a smaller format is preferable. A weighty tome with umpteen pictures is more likely to require the larger 'coffee table' format.

Considering the dust jacket

If you are looking to produce small hardback books with a dust jacket, a potential constraint worth considering is the size of paper used by copy shops. They tend to cite A3, although a slightly larger paper is used so that it can be trimmed and presented to the client as A3. Your chosen book size must allow for the flaps of the dust jacket to wrap around.

Keeping within this size should ensure that the print cost (not including any design you require) is no more than £50 for 25 dust jackets, with the unit price decreasing thereafter. If larger paper is required, there is likely to be an overhead of several hundred pounds, resulting in an extortionate price per dust jacket unless many hundreds of copies are ordered.

Q: What do the above constraints mean in terms of dimensions and the number of words?

A: For a book of anything up to 300 pages printed on 80 or 90 GSM paper, page dimensions should be no greater than 150×210mm. Side and bottom margins should be at least 15mm, with 25mm allowed for the top margin. Using a font size of 11 (based on Times Roman), this will be sufficient for a book of up of 120,000 words. For pages of pictures, reduce the word count by 400 words per page.

Choosing the font

The main body of text

The style of font is one of the most important factors in the presentation of any document, as anyone familiar with word processing will know. Getting the right font for your book is even more important and Word has more than enough fonts to provide ample choice. For those with especially demanding requirements, plenty more fonts are available on the Internet.

The size of font is also crucial and will be one of the factors determining the size of your book, as discussed above. It is worth taking time to experiment with combinations of font size and line spacing, the latter of which is discussed below

You might opt for a larger font to make your book easier for those with poor eyesight, but be careful that it is not so large that people feel they are being patronised.

Headings

A larger font can be used for chapter headings and any sub-headings, or a different style of font completely. You may even prefer CAPITALS or SMALL CAPITALS. Again, experimenting is the best advice, but once you've made your decision, be consistent throughout the book.

Avoid being too clever

Word processors have so many options for font style, size and clever tricks that some people get carried away. It is fine to use italics from time to time, or even, at a push, the occasional <u>underlining</u>. Personally, I am not keen on **bold** in a book, and **ADDING SHADOW** is definitely going too far.

By all means have fun experimenting, but keep the manuscript plain and simple and, above all, be consistent.

Designing the page layout

Page layout and page size are intimately related, as layout has a direct impact on how people read and enjoy a book. Nearly two years was spent on research before *The Guardian* newspaper changed its size and style, because it was appreciated that the page layout would have a huge impact on readership.

In using a word processor such as Word, there are *at least* the following to consider.

Understanding orientation

The vast majority of books are produced in portrait format – that is, they are taller than they are wide. Landscape books – being wider than they are tall – are generally reserved for picture books and large coffee-table type presentations.

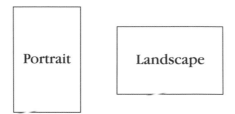

Within a book, it may be necessary to change the orientation of a single page to accommodate a landscape picture, a complicated table, or several photos next to each other. Within Word, section breaks must be used (Insert menu, Break, and choose a continuous break), and then the orientation of that page can be altered from File and Page Setup. However, you must then change the following pages back to the normal orientation, so that the rest of the book reads as standard.

Ensure that you deal consistently with landscape pages so that they face the same way throughout the book. This is especially important for pages produced independently and then slotted into the manuscript, like a family tree.

Setting the margins – four of them

The top and bottom margins can be left blank, but can also be home for headers, footers and page numbers. Word will allow you only to set margins that work within the size of the paper you have specified, and the size of the paper that your printer will print on. In the File menu, choose Page Setup and select Margins to change the size. The right and left hand margins should not be too narrow, as we like to have somewhere to put our hands without obscuring the text! If you are having your page sizes cut down from a larger sheet, make sure the top and bottom margins are wide enough to allow for the trimming, and also that they are in proportion to the side margins.

Considering headers and footers

Some books, like this one, have the book title on the top of the left hand page and the chapter title on the right. These could equally appear at the bottom of the page. Positioning is changed in Page Setup, the content being altered by choosing Header and Footer from the View menu and then clicking directly on the header area as it appears on the screen.

Inserting page numbers

Traditionally, page numbers are alphanumeric, although often the prelims (see Chapter 13) are found with Roman numerals, or sometimes even letters.

Numbering a single Word document is simple, by choosing Page Numbers from the Insert menu. However, Word documents that have section or page breaks follow specific rules for numbering that can be confusing to the uninitiated. A page number can always be altered by double clicking on it as it appears on the screen page, and altering the number. This also gives access to menus changing its positioning and sequencing.

Sequencing is important if you have inserted a page break and wish to start numbers afresh, or to instruct all numbers to follow on from the previous numbers. If you are attempting a complicated document with breaks, then my advice would be to leave the page numbering until the very end – make it practically the last thing you do before you head off to the printer!

Allowing for a gutter

The gutter is the area at the binding edge of the page which printers leave to allow for the binding. Small documents do not need a gutter, especially if they have large margins. However, thick books, or books which you take to a professional printer or binder, may need a small gutter. Word can automatically place this at the correct edge – choose Page Layout from the File menu.

Justification

Simply put, this relates to how the words sit on a line.

This is right justified – the words sit flush to the right.

This is centred.

This sentence, being quite long, is fully justified and looks rather neat because, as you can see, the paragraph forms a straight line on both the right and the left hand sides. This book is fully justified, the word processor automatically inserting consistent spacing between words to ensure a straight line on both edges of the page.

This paragraph is not justified and consequently the words do not align on the right hand side of the page. You need to decide which you prefer for your book, but whatever you decide follow the general rule of being consistent. As you can see from the various styles here, the page looks clumsy and is irritating for the reader when you mix and match your choices.

The justification options can be chosen from the small icons at the top of the Word screen, or from the Paragraph option in the Format menu. All but the most unusual books use either left or full justification. However, centreing text is often used for titles, headings, and possibly poems, for example.

Deciding on spacing

A typesetter has numerous options as to how letters, words, lines, paragraphs, pictures and other items are all spaced from each other. Most word processors also provide more options than you require for producing your own life story, so we shall consider only the most important.

Line spacing

Altering the space between lines has an amazing impact on the readability of the text. When printing the early versions of your manuscript, it is worth using double or at least 1.5 line spacing (Format menu and then Paragraph). This allows you to study the text carefully, and make any marks for corrections or alterations.

Spacing of 1.5 is clearly too childish for the final version of your book, although the size of this paragraph at 0.8 is much too tight, making it very hard work to read. You would not be able to struggle through too many lines of this before getting a headache!

Whilst the default of the word processor will be set at '1', you might want to experiment with a decimal point or two larger as it can be very pleasing on the eye, particularly for readers with less than perfect sight. Select the 'multiple' option from the line spacing window in Format – Paragraph and then specify a factor in the box next to that window, something between 1 and 1.5. The digit of line spacing (1, 1.5, double, or whatever) always relates to the maximum character height, which you will specify through the size of your font.

Paragraph spacing

Paragraphs can simply start on a new line, but you might like to change the gap between paragraphs so that they are slightly different from the gaps between lines. A double 'return' will achieve this, or you can be more specific via the Format – Paragraph menu, specifying the space either before or after every paragraph.

If you prefer to indent the first line of your paragraphs, this can be achieved via Format, Paragraph and choosing First Line in the Special section.

Character spacing

As laying out a book becomes more technical, so do the options. Modern word processors do all the spacing between characters for you automatically, according to rules established by the designer of the font. These can be changed (choose Format menu, then the Font option, and click the Character Spacing tab), but this is only really necessary in extreme circumstances – for example, when you have a long sentence that runs onto the next page by only one word, but you would rather it finishes on the last full page. Select the text in that paragraph and condense the character spacing by a fraction, and hey presto... and no one will be any the wiser!

Widows and orphans

Widows and orphans are bits of text that have got separated. A paragraph that runs from the bottom of one page to the top of the next may leave just one line on that second page. This stranded 'orphan' can look messy. Alternatively, a new paragraph may be seven or eight lines long, but because it starts at the bottom of the page, it leaves an isolated 'widow' line that can look silly. If you wish to avoid widows and orphans, the computer can automatically move text from one page to another, ensuring a minimum of two lines appearing together. In Word, this is done through Format, Paragraph and then clicking the Line and Page Breaks option, where the Widow/Orphan control box can be ticked.

Dealing with specialist sections

Prelims and appendices

The same rules apply for prelims and appendices as discussed in Chapter 13. However, with a word processor you now have many more options regarding their presentation. As with the rest of the book, set them out simply and cleanly. It is advisable to use separate pages. You can number the prelims separately, perhaps using Roman numerals, but it is far easier to count them in the run of the book, and more convenient if the book is to be produced by a copy shop.

The index

Options exist within Word to flag certain words or names to assist with an index. You might want to use this for more formal or academic books, but for private life stories it is unusual to do so. The danger of including an index is that people immediately look up their name to see what has been written about them and not read the rest of the book. Additionally, they can compare the number of times their name appears or, worse still, see that that have been overlooked altogether!

Family trees

Most word processors are not ideal for designing family trees, although there is plenty of software available for this purpose. The problem with family trees is as stated in Chapter 13: they cannot be updated once bound within a book, and unless they fit onto a single page they can be unwieldy to use. If you wish to produce a family tree, treat it as a separate project to be kept alongside your book.

Incorporating photos

Photographs bring a life story… to life! Computers make this much easier and more professional, although remember the warnings about how memory-hungry pictures can be. As with any computer work, save your files regularly, and make back-ups, in case anything goes wrong.

Scanning the images

Scanning is a fairly simple process. All software packages have slight variations, but it is usually a case of placing the image face down on the scanner (as you would on a photocopier), and then clicking the scan button. Some provide a preview of the images, so by clicking the mouse and dragging a box, you can highlight exactly what you wish to scan.

Choosing the correct resolution

You should be presented with a choice of resolution for scan-ning the image. The resolution is usually measured in the dots per inch, or 'dpi'. The higher the number, the better the quality of the photograph when it is reproduced. However, there are several points that must be taken into considera-tion. Pictures scanned at extremely high resolution take up an enormous amount of memory and so are very slow to handle with normal computers.

The resolution of your pictures need only be as good as the resolution of the printer you are going to use – it is a waste of time scanning at 1200 dpi if your printer has a maximum res-olution output of 300 dpi. 150 dpi is too low for a final print, and 600 dpi is more than good enough, so anywhere from 300 dpi upwards will produce good results.

When the image has been scanned, you often have the oppor-tunity to edit the picture. A good tip at this stage is to crop out any extra material you don't wish to reproduce in the final document – for example, the frame around a photo-graph, or large amounts of background that are not relevant to the picture you want to show and which would distract from the image.

Selecting the format

Once you are happy with what you have scanned, you will need to save the image. Programs usually allow you to specify in what format the image is to be saved. The root of the file-name determines the format – the three letters that come after the dot following the name you give the picture. The computer usually inserts the three letters; you just have to choose the format. So, Granny.jpg is in the JPEG format, eiffeltower.tif is in the TIFF format, and buckinghampalace.gif is in the GIF format.

As computers have developed, numerous different formats have been created for saving digital images. Some have specific uses and are best suited to a particular environment – for example, JPEGs and GIFs are most frequently found on the Internet. The different formats handle data in different ways, and some image types are not always compatible with other software programs. The best options are either JPEGs at a fairly high resolution, or TIFF files. Practically all software packages can use these, so there should be little compatibility problem if you are taking your document to be printed elsewhere.

Practice makes perfect

Scanning is a fairly time-consuming process, and it takes a while to get it right, so spend time practising. Also, most programs allow you to do many things to a picture – brighten it, change the contrast, even remove scratches and red-eye, so have a play and see what you come up with. You still have the original, so don't be scared about harming the digital image – you can always re-scan and start again.

Placing pictures in the text

Word allows pictures to be placed via the Insert – Picture – From File menus; you choose the image that you have previously saved and drop it into the text. The picture can then be centred or justified, as with text, and enlarged or shrunk by clicking on the square dots on the corner of the image and dragging accordingly. This is one of the great advantages of doing images digitally on computer – in theory you can have them where you want and in the size you want.

When you click on a picture, the computer usually highlights it with a box which has eight dots around it – one on each corner, and one on the middle of each side. To change a picture's size, click and drag the corner dots – this will preserve the aspect ratio of the picture (that is, the ratio between the height and the width of the picture will remain the same, however big or small it becomes). If you don't do this, and click and drag on one of the side dots, you can end up with images resembling something out of a hall of mirrors – stretched faces, or squashed people!

Cropping photos

To crop a picture, click on the image; a picture menu should then appear, from which you can choose the crop icon (two crosses on a diagonal) and cut out parts of the picture you don't want. One customer did this on her wedding picture to her ex-husband... deliberately!

Experimenting

If you are feeling adventurous, there are many more options for playing with photos – place your cursor over the image, then right-click the mouse and explore the options you are presented with. If anything goes wrong, press CTRL-Z, and the document will be restored to the status before the last option – a very useful tip to know!

Pictures look best with good margins around them. A brief caption is also usually helpful – especially for the uninitiated who cannot tell Great Uncle Tom from Great Aunt Mavis!

Getting carried away

Too many pictures can be a problem – we all have thousands these days, but it is best to be selective. It must be remembered that this is a life story, not a photo album, and you don't want all your hard work in writing to be overshadowed just because you have dozens of pictures of grandchildren and a sophisticated scanner. Those reading your book will prefer to see pictures of *you*, and older pictures are invariably more interesting than recent ones.

Looking after the computer

Once you have a few pictures in your document, the size of the file will increase rapidly and the computer will slow down. Save the document, and if it becomes really slow, break the book down into separate files for each chapter – then each file will only be a fraction of the final size. If you do this, remember to start the new chapter with the correct page number!

Incorporating family trees

There are a great many ways of representing family trees, mapping out where you came from and who you are related to, but there is one problem... they can be incredibly complicated. This complexity has implications when it comes to printing, but there are a number of ways to handle this.

Some of the most beautiful family trees are hand-drawn. These carefully crafted charts possess a lot of charm and preserve not just the information but something of the author too. However, this requires skill and careful planning.

Family tree software

For those of us with less artistic ability, computers provide a fine alternative, particularly if the family tree is to be amended from time to time. Simple family trees can be constructed with Microsoft Word, using the drawing tools and inserting text boxes with the relevant information. These boxes can then be joined up with the line tools. Whilst effective, this approach can be very fiddly, and managing a mass of information on one page is tricky.

Better still are the many fine and increasingly wide selection of bespoke family tree software programmes. They all have their own bells and whistles, but if you are seriously interested in family trees, it is probably worth purchasing one. The starting price for a decent programme is about £30, and they are fairly easy to install and navigate. Make sure they can generate files with the .ged file extension, as these are interchangeable between most programmes. Family Tree Maker is one such programme, and the deluxe edition allows access and search on internet genealogy databases.

Remember, almost as soon as you commit a family tree to paper, it will be out of date – a new grandchild will be born, there will be a marriage, death or divorce, a distant relation will complain that you got their birth date wrong, and a second cousin once removed will pop out of the woodwork. So be prepared!

Designing the cover

If you have enjoyed designing and producing the rest of your book, there is no reason why you should not design your own cover. If a copy shop is producing your books, they will be happy to provide you with the required specifications.

Should you prefer, the copy shop will be happy to design your cover for a modest fee. A single image, or a collage of three or four pictures, should not be onerous on the pocket, although costs will increase with the complexity of your requirements.

And finally . . .

Enjoying the project
It is hoped that writing your book will have been a highly enjoyable process. If your enthusiasm for producing it starts to wane or you feel bogged down with the technology,

consider seeking external help, either from a friend or a specialist company. Having assistance to produce your book can be more enjoyable once the headache of having to work everything out for yourself has been removed.

Writing your life story should be an immensely satisfying and stimulating project. Ensure that it remains so right up to the moment of opening a bottle of bubbly to celebrate its launch.

Checklist

- Ensure consistency in the size and style of chapter headings.
- Check spellings in the photo captions if they have been added since proofreading the final draft of your book.
- Before your book goes to print, check the final proofs thoroughly, paying particular attention to the overall appearance of each page and how pleasing it is to the eye. What you fail to alter now will appear in the finished book.

Assignments

- If the books are being printed by a third party, ask to see a sample of the quality of photos you can expect, so there are no nasty surprises when you receive your precious books.
- Give some thought to the design of the book cover, allowing your mind to wander regarding what you would like to see. After all, having come this far, you may as well get what you want!
- Seek advice from the copy shop about the book cover or dust jacket, and ask for sample copies and a quote for printing and design costs.

Advice from Others Who Have Written 18

This chapter includes snippets of advice from those who have already written their life stories. Not everything will coincide with the ideas you have for your own writing, but hopefully some of the advice will be helpful.

* * * * *

When you seriously contemplate writing your life story, start collecting details, particularly from elderly relatives or friends. Often, a supposedly minor detail can provide considerable interest!

Travers Johnson

I know that the most important thing I've ever done is to write my life story. Future generations will now know who I am, where I came from, and what I was like, warts and all. I would like to think all who read it will discover that I have another side to my personality... a quieter one!

Olga Moorhouse

The written word is like painting; you bring that story to life with colour, movement, mood and emphasis.

Shirley Martins

When out for a walk on your own, or when travelling, it is surprising what things can pop into the mind. Carry a notebook at all times and jot down straightaway what you remember or feel, because thoughts can slip out of the mind again as easily as they slip in.

Arda Lees

Start by numbering your pages – it helps to catalogue your progress, saves pages getting out of order and is encouraging to see how much you have written.

Barry Barrett

Having clarified in your own mind the reason for writing your story, then decide the audience for it, i.e. the family, including siblings, close friends, former colleagues, etc. Such a decision might determine how you express yourself, and the need to avoid hurts, misunderstanding or even libel.

Dr Bill Barton

Keep an eye on your main story, but digress into anecdotes, which will humanise the tale and make it interesting.

Leonard Hall

Whatever your target market, but especially if it is your own family, let them know in some detail how the world has changed in your lifetime. The last fifty years have seen more changes – in domestic life and in general – than the previous thousand; the next fifty will probably see the rate of change speed up even more, so there will be great interest in hearing 'how it was'.

Sir John Quinton

My advice to someone who is thinking of writing his or her life story is, don't delay. It is a good project, both therapeutic and educational, but most of all it is a wonderful legacy to leave for your family, especially any grandchildren.

Stella Wills

Don't forget to use whatever references you have to hand: photo albums, diaries, reports written or special papers published – they all help to trigger memories.

Dr Bill Barton

Try to make your writing humorous and be prepared to laugh at your own mistakes and misfortunes.

Mary Robinson

A computer is excellent for storing information, but a strong folder with a wallet should be an early purchase. This is invaluable for holding items like photos, newspaper or periodical cuttings, interesting or official letters, identity or warrant cards, licences or official passes, etc as well as your own notes.

Travers Johnson

In describing events, write as fully and descriptively as possible. It makes bald facts come alive and very much more interesting.

Arda Lees

If you are using a word processor, save your work as you go along, and especially when you leave it to go shopping, etc. Set yourself a limited target and don't become overtired – that's the way costly mistakes can occur… and I speak from personal experience.

Barry Barrett

(Barry inadvertently deleted the file of his entire life story and there was no backup – so he wrote it all again… all 50,000 words!)

Be prepared to titillate your reader, encouraging them to read on.

Shirley Martins

If there are any tricky areas to write about, or anything over which you are at all concerned, check with the people mentioned that they are happy with what is in the text. More than likely they will be delighted, but it might save any potential awkwardness once the book is in print, even with a limited circulation.

Elizabeth Coxon-Taylor

Divide your writing into periods of your life so that the reader will not be confused as to what happened when. When satisfied, write them out in full.

Mary Robinson

A dictionary and thesaurus are helpful, and I found that looking at old snapshots was a good memory jogger.

Stella Wills

I didn't just write about facts. I learned not to be afraid to convey my feelings and emotions to paper. If you can do this, it will reveal the real 'you', which is probably what your children and great-grandchildren really want to know about you.

Arda Lees

Writing my life story is one of my finest achievements – that beautiful leather-bound volume holds a chronicle for my family.

Shirley Martins

In writing about relatives near and far, jot down a simple family tree to help you with names and dates. It is important that details are checked as errors can easily slip in, resulting in a rap across the knuckles from your favourite aunt!

Travers Johnson

You will overlook many things on the first run through, so let each chapter 'rest' for a while, making brief notes as memories come back to you.

Sir John Quinton

Give a full account of when you were young, then if your grandchildren read it they may have a completely different perception of you – mine did!

Barry Barrett

Look at old photographs for the memories they evoke, and if the picture includes yourself, try to remember the occasion. Looking closely at the styles and fashions of what you wore, the hairstyles, etc can often jog your memory on the small details and remind you of an occasion you had forgotten. Thinking on these lines often brings back more recollections of people and places long gone from the mind.

Arda Lees

You may not be wholly uncritical, but take care not to give serious offence.

Leonard Hall

Use time wisely – do not get stressed, overtired or bored. Switch off for a few days if necessary.

Elizabeth Coxon-Taylor

Don't think about the number of words you are going to write. Instead, write about everything you can remember, ask someone to read it through, and then decide together what (if anything) needs to be taken out. It is far better to write too much than too little.

Barbara Cox

Focus on the 'good deeds' in the family, and forget the bad ones.

Travers Johnson

Don't tell anyone what you're doing (they will think it's a five-minute wonder anyway). They will then be even more astounded when you tell them you have completed it.

Barry Barrett

Discipline is essential, allowing you a certain time in the day to think, write and collate information. The pure thrill of seeing your words and paragraphs emerge into that first chapter almost becomes addictive. This is a cathartic exercise that requires stamina, perseverance and a magical sense of humour.

Shirley Martins

During the writing of my book I found peace and tranquillity, and enjoyment in reminiscing through the good and sad times. People who have read it have boosted my ego.

Stella Wills

Include as many life incidents and anecdotes as possible, to lighten up the narrative.

Sir John Quinton

Read autobiographies from your library to get ideas of what is interesting to you to help in your writing.

Elizabeth Coxon-Taylor

The writing does not have to be of a high literary standard – it just needs to come from the heart. Write as you would tell it. Be yourself.

Arda Lees

When writing, I have laughed a lot and cried a lot! I still keep a copy of the book by my chair, and I read it when I have a quiet minute – even though I wrote it, I can't believe that it is me! I've loved it and would do it all again!

Olga Moorhouse

To conclude this chapter, Brian Hacon has composed a little rhyme:

'Me write a story? What a laugh!'
Is what most people say.
But just a moment – don't say 'No',
There just might be a way.

You've lived your life, so know well
That there is no one better,
To tell the tale and set it down,
Accurate to the letter.

Break down your life, just as it was,
Childhood, youth, perhaps marriage,
Schooldays, holidays, and while at work
Driving a horse and carriage.

All lives are different, none the same;
Each person is unique;
Maybe an unimportant life to you
Has more interest than you think.

Your friends and family will enjoy
The story you relate;
Surprise them all, just let them know
Life hasn't been so sedate.

Make it worthwhile and go for broke,
Give it all you've got.
Enjoy the buzz of your life in print,
Before you go to pot!

I've done it now, put down my pen;
My story is complete.
I can sit and enjoy my life anew,
As I put up my feet.

Reactions have been wholesome,
Surprisingly sublime!
Who knows? I might bore them all again
With a sequel in ten years' time.

Brian Hacon

Author's Postscript

Writing your life story, and that of the special people you've encountered along the way, is one of the most precious things anyone can do. Consequently, I am keen that this book be as thorough and accessible as possible and would welcome any suggestions for improvement.

To my mind, I have the best job in the world – helping ordinary people to write their life stories for their friends, families and, most importantly, for themselves to enjoy. Of course, I am still waiting to meet that elusive 'ordinary' person.

Over the past 17 years I have had the immense privilege of helping dozens of very special people with their own autobiographies, and there is now a team of us throughout the country who provide this 'hand-holding' service, whether the would-be writer has yet to put pen to paper or has largely written a manuscript and requires assistance with tidying it up and producing a few copies for family and friends.

A few years ago whilst running a 'Writing Your Life Story' seminar, I was approached by a lady who had attended the previous year's course. She presented me with a copy of the book she had written in the interim. I was delighted and treasure it along with the others I have helped produce. If this book has helped in your own writing, I would be delighted to receive an autographed copy of your own book (should you have one to spare) to read and keep with my special collection.

Thank you for reading this book, and if you feel that it has been of any assistance, please pass it on to a friend.

Good Luck with your own writing!

Michael Oke

www.boundbiographies.com

Appendix 1
Reference Materials

Imperial/Decimal currency converter

Imperial	Decimal
1d	$\frac{1}{2}$p
2d	1p
3d	1p
4d	$1\frac{1}{2}$p
5d	2p
6d	$2\frac{1}{2}$p
7d	3p
8d	$3\frac{1}{2}$p
9d	4p
10d	4p
11d	$4\frac{1}{2}$p
12d (one shilling)	5p

Imperial	Decimal
1 shilling	5p
2 shillings	10p
3 shillings	15p
4 shillings	20p
5 shillings	25p
6 shillings	30p
7 shillings	35p
8 shillings	40p
9 shillings	45p
10 shillings	50p
11 shillings	55p
12 shillings	60p
13 shillings	65p
14 shillings	70p
15 shillings	75p
16 shillings	80p
17 shillings	85p
18 shillings	90p
19 shillings	95p
20 shillings	£1.00

Comparison of prices 1930–1978
Prices in decimal currency.

	1931–40	1941–44	1945–50	1951–60	1961–70	1978
Bread 1lb	1p	1p	$1\frac{1}{4}$p	$2\frac{1}{2}$p	4p	17p
Butter 1lb	6p	5p	$6\frac{1}{2}$p	10p	20p	68p
Cheese 1lb	$4\frac{1}{2}$p	$5\frac{1}{2}$p	5p	$12\frac{1}{2}$p	17p	64p
Eggs per doz	$7\frac{1}{2}$p	$10\frac{1}{2}$p	$12\frac{1}{2}$p	23p	37p	51p
Sugar 1lb	1p	$1\frac{1}{2}$p	1p	1p	3p	30p
Potatoes (14lb)	11p	12p	14p	24p	35p	98p

	1931–40	1941–44	1945–50	1951–60	1961–70	1978
Bacon 1lb	5p	7p	$8^{1}/_{2}$p	12p	21p	82p
Beef 1lb	$4^{1}/_{2}$p	$5^{1}/_{2}$p	7p	8p	14p	84p
Tea $^{1}/_{4}$lb	3p	$5^{1}/_{2}$p	$6^{1}/_{2}$p	9p	9p	24p
Coffee $^{1}/_{4}$lb	8p	10p	10p	15p	18p	£1.00
Cigarettes	6p	11p	16p	22p	29p	70p
Pint of beer	3p	5p	$6^{1}/_{2}$p	6p	6p	30p
Whisky	65p	£1.10	£1.70	£1.80	£2.42$^{1}/_{2}$	£4.29
Shoes	£1.00	£1.25	£1.50	£3.00	£4.50	£19.00
Stockings/tights	20p	15p	15p	20p	25p	60p
Postage stamp	1p	1p	$1^{1}/_{2}$p	$1^{1}/_{2}$p	2p	9p
The Times	1p	1p	1p	$1^{1}/_{2}$p	5p	15p
Daily Mail	$^{1}/_{2}$p	$^{1}/_{2}$p	$^{1}/_{2}$p	1p	$2^{1}/_{2}$p	9p
Radio	£20	war	£25	£30	£90	–
TV set	n/a	war	£80	£80	£90	–
Cooker	£7	war	£12	£23	£50	£157
Refrigerator	£50	war	£50	£50	£60	£100
Vacuum cleaner	£19	war	£30	£35	£40	£75
Sewing machine	£20	war	£35	£40	£60	£90
Bicycle	£6	war	£12	£20	£30	£63
Family car	£235	war	£597	£800	£927	£2,328
Coal (per ton)	£1.35	£1.70	£3.60	£7.66	£15.00	£48.00
Petrol (gallon)	8p	$10^{1}/_{2}$p	$11^{1}/_{2}$p	21p	25p	80p
House 3-bed semi	£750	£800	£2,200	£2,750	£6,000	£19,500
Income (weekly)						
Skilled male	£5.00	£5.00	£6.50	£11.00	£20.00	£83.50
Unskilled male	£4.00	£4.00	£5.00	£7.00	£13.00	£43.00
State Retirement Pension						
Single	50p	50p	£1.30	£2.50	£5.00	£19.50
Married	50p	50p	£2.10	£4.00	£8.10	£31.50
Income Tax (in the £)	24p	50p	46p	45p	40.25p	33p

With kind permission from *The What it Cost the Day before Yesterday Book* by Dr Harold Priestly, published by Kenneth Mason Publications Ltd, The Book Barn, Westbourne, Hants.

Anniversaries

1	paper
2	cotton
3	leather
4	linen
5	wood
6	iron
7	wool
8	bronze
9	pottery
10	tin
11	steel
12	silk
13	lace
14	ivory
15	crystal
20	china
25	silver
30	pearl
35	coral
40	ruby
45	sapphire
50	gold
55	emerald
60	diamond
65	blue sapphire
70	platinum
75	diamond (historically)
75	double diamond (contemporary)

British Prime Ministers since 1900

25 June 1895	Marquess of Salisbury	Conservative
12 July 1902	Arthur Balfour	Conservative
5 December 1905	Henry Campbell-Bannerman	Liberal
7 April 1908	Herbert Asquith	Liberal (Coalition Government 1915)
7 December 1916	David Lloyd George	Liberal (Coalition Government)
23 October 1922	Andrew Bonar Law	Conservative
22 May 1923	Stanley Baldwin	Conservative
22 January 1924	James Ramsay MacDonald	Labour
4 November 1924	Stanley Baldwin	Conservative
5 June 1929	James Ramsay MacDonald	Labour
24 August 1931	James Ramsay MacDonald	National Labour (National Government)
7 June 1935	Stanley Baldwin	Conservative (National Government)
28 May 1937	Neville Chamberlain	Conservative (National Government)
10 May 1940	Winston Churchill	Conservative (Coalition Government)
23 May 1945	Winston Churchill	Conservative (Caretaker Government)
26 July 1945	Clement Attlee	Labour
26 October 1951	Winston Churchill	Conservative
6 April 1955	Sir Anthony Eden	Conservative
10 January 1957	Harold Macmillan	Conservative
19 October 1963	Sir Alec Douglas-Home	Conservative
16 October 1964	Harold Wilson	Labour
19 June 1970	Edward Heath	Conservative
4 March 1974	Harold Wilson	Labour
5 April 1976	James Callaghan	Labour
4 May 1979	Margaret Thatcher	Conservative
28 November 1990	John Major	Conservative
2 May 1997	Tony Blair	Labour
27 June 2007	Gordon Brown	Labour

Royal Events since 1930

29 November 1934	Prince George, Duke of Kent, marries Princess Marina of Greece
6 May 1935	Silver Jubilee of King George V and Queen Mary
20 January 1936	Death of King George V
21 January 1936	Edward VIII proclaimed King
11 December 1936	Edward VIII renounced the throne to marry Mrs Wallis Simpson
12 December 1936	George VI proclaimed King
12 May 1937	Coronation of King George VI
20 November 1947	Wedding of Princess Elizabeth and Lieutenant Philip Mountbatten
14 November 1948	Birth of Charles Philip Arthur George
15 August 1950	Birth of Anne Elizabeth Alice Louise
6 February 1952	Death of King George VI
8 February 1952	Elizabeth II proclaimed Queen upon her return from Kenya
25 March 1953	Death of Queen Mary, widow of George V
2 June 1953	Coronation of Queen Elizabeth II
19 February 1960	Birth of Andrew Christian Edward
6 May 1960	Wedding of Princess Margaret and Anthony Armstrong-Jones
10 March 1964	Birth of Edward Antony Richard Louis
1 July 1969	Prince Charles' Investiture as Prince of Wales
28 May 1972	Death of Duke of Windsor, ex-King Edward VIII
14 November 1973	Wedding of Princess Anne to Captain Mark Phillips
6 June 1977	Queen Elizabeth II's Silver Jubilee
29 July 1981	Wedding of Prince Charles and Lady Diana Spencer
21 June 1982	Birth of William Arthur Philip Louis
15 September 1984	Birth of Henry Charles Albert David – 'Harry'
23 July 1986	Wedding of Prince Andrew and Sarah Ferguson
6 June 1992	Queen Elizabeth II celebrates 40 years as monarch
20 November 1992	Fire at Windsor Castle

12 December 1992	Wedding of Princess Anne to Commander Tim Laurence
31 August 1997	Death of Diana, Princess of Wales
20 December 1997	Golden Wedding Anniversary of Queen Elizabeth and Prince Philip
19 June 1999	Wedding of Prince Edward and Sophie Rhys-Jones
4 August 2000	Queen Elizabeth, the Queen Mother's 100th birthday
30 March 2002	Death of Queen Elizabeth, the Queen Mother
9 April 2005	Wedding of Prince Charles and Camilla Parker Bowles

Music Hits – 1930–2000

1930	*Puttin' On the Ritz*	Fred Lewis
	On the Sunny Side of the Street	Ted Lewis and His Band
	Valentine	Maurice Chevalier
	She's My Secret Passion	Ambrose
1931	*Sally*	Gracie Fields
	Dream a Little Dream of Me	Ozzie Nelson
	Goodnight Sweetheart	Al Bowlly
	Lazy River	Louis Armstrong
1932	*Brother, Can You Spare a Dime?*	Bing Crosby
	Love is the Sweetest Thing	Al Bowlly
	Mad Dogs and Englishmen	Noel Coward
	Mah Lindy Lou	Paul Robeson
1933	*Stormy Weather*	Ethel Water
	Night and Day	Eddie Duchin
	Lazy Bones	Don Redman's Band
	Shadow Waltz	Bing Crosby
1934	*On the Good Ship Lollipop*	Shirley Temple
	You're the Top	Paul Whiteman and His Orchestra
	Dancing On The Ceiling	Jessie Matthews
	Smoke Gets in Your Eyes	Turner Layton

1935	*Blue Moon*	Glen Gray and the Casa Loma Orchestra
	Red Sails in the Sunset	Guy Lombardo and His Royal Canadians
	Chasing Shadows	The Dorsey Brothers Orchestra
	The Lady in Red	Louis Prima
1936	*When I'm Cleaning Windows*	George Formby
	The Music Goes Round and Round	Tommy Dorsey
	A Fine Romance	Fred Astaire
	Pennies from Heaven	Bing Crosby
1937	*September in the Rain*	Guy Lombardo
	Goodnight, My Love	Benny Goodman
	That Old Feeling	Shep Fields
	Peace in the Valley	Mahalia Jackson
1938	*A-Tisket, A-Tasket*	Ella Fitzgerald
	Begin the Beguine	Artie Shaw
	Cry, Baby, Cry	Larry Clinton
	Bei Mir Bist Du Schoen	Andrews Sisters
1939	*Over the Rainbow*	Judy Garland
	Stairway to the Stars	Glenn Miller
	Jeepers Creepers	Al Donohue
	Scatter-Brain	Frankie Masters
1940	*A Nightingale Sang in Berkeley Square*	Judy Campbell
	In the Mood	Glenn Miller
	Playmates	Hal Kemp and The Smoothies
	I'll Never Smile Again	Tommy Dorsey
1941	*White Cliffs of Dover*	Vera Lynn
	Boogie Woogie Bugle Boy	Andrews Sisters
	Chattanooga Choo Choo	Glenn Miller
	There I Go	Vaughn Monroe

1942	*We'll Meet Again*	Vera Lynn
	White Christmas	Bing Crosby
	Don't Sit Under the Apple Tree	Andrews Sisters
	Jingle, Jangle, Jingle	Kay Kyser
1943	*When the Lights Go On Again*	Vaughn Monroe
	You'll Never Know	Dick Haymes
	As Time Goes By	Rudy Vallee
	Taking a Chance on Love	Benny Goodman
1944	*Mairzy Doats*	Merry Macs
	Swinging on a Star	Bing Crosby
	Long Ago (And Far Away)	Perry Como
	I'll Get By	Harry James
1945	*Sentimental Journey*	Les Brown and Doris Day
	Till the End of Time	Perry Como
	Chickery Chick	Sammy Kaye
	Doctor, Lawyer, Indian Chief	Betty Hutton
1946	*September in the Rain*	Frankie Laine
	We'll Gather Lilacs	Geraldo and his Orchestra
	Winter Wonderland	Perry Como
	Blue Skies	Bing Crosby
1947	*April Showers*	Al Jolson
	In the Still of the night	Jo Stafford
	Night and Day	Frank Sinatra
	Singing the Blues	Frankie Laine
1948	*Deck of Cards*	Phil Harris
	It's Magic	Doris Day
	Rosetta	Frankie Laine
	Nature Boy	Nat King Cole
1949	*Baby It's Cold Outside*	Dinah Shore and Buddy Clark
	O Sole Mio	Mario Lanza
	Some Enchanted Evening	Perry Como
	Goodnight Irene	The Weavers

1950	*Mona Lisa*	Nat King Cole
	The Third Man Theme	Anton Karas
	Music! Music! Music!	Teresa Brewer
	I Wanna Be Loved	Andrews Sisters
1951	*If*	Perry Como
	Too Young	Nat King Cole
	On Top of Old Smoky	The Weavers
	Lullaby of Broadway	Doris Day
1952	*You Belong to Me*	Jo Stafford
	Here in My Heart	Al Martino
	Unforgettable	Nat King Cole
	Wheel of Fortune	Kay Starr
1953	*Don't Let the Stars Get in Your Eyes*	Perry Como
	Look at That Girl	Guy Mitchell
	I Believe	Frankie Laine
	(How Much Is) That Doggie in the Window	Lita Roza
1954	*Secret Love*	Doris Day
	Three Coins in the Fountain	Frank Sinatra
	This Ole House	Rosemary Clooney
	Oh Mein Papa	Eddie Calvert
1955	*Rock Around the Clock*	Bill Haley and his Comets
	Rose Marie	Slim Whitman
	Give Me Your Word	Tennessee Ernie Ford
	Unchained Melody	Jimmy Young
1956	*Memories are Made of This*	Dean Martin
	Whatever Will Be Will Be	Doris Day
	Just Walkin' in the Rain	Johnnie Ray
	No Other Love	Ronnie Hilton

1957	*Mary's Boy Child*	Harry Belafonte
	Young Love	Tab Hunter
	All Shook Up	Elvis Presley
	Diana	Paul Anka
1958	*Who's Sorry Now?*	Connie Francis
	Great Balls of Fire	Jerry Lee Lewis
	Jailhouse Rock	Elvis Presley
	Magic Moments	Perry Como
1959	*Living Doll*	Cliff Richard
	Only Sixteen	Craig Douglas
	Smoke Gets in Your Eyes	The Platters
	Dream Lover	Bobby Darin
1960	*Cathy's Clown*	The Everly Brothers
	My Old Man's a Dustman	Lonnie Donegan
	Apache	The Shadows
	Tell Laura I Love Her	Ricky Valance
1961	*Walkin' Back to Happiness*	Helen Shapiro
	Wooden Heart	Elvis Presley
	Runaway	Del Shannon
	Moon River	Danny Williams
1962	*The Young Ones*	Cliff Richard
	I Remember You	Frank Ifield
	Telstar	The Tornados
	Return to Sender	Elvis Presley
1963	*From Me to You*	The Beatles
	You'll Never Walk Alone	Gerry and the Pacemakers
	Summer Holiday	Cliff Richard
	She Loves You	The Beatles
1964	*House of the Rising Sun*	The Animals
	You're My World	Cilla Black
	A Hard Day's Night	The Beatles
	Baby Love	The Supremes

1965	*It's Not Unusual*	Tom Jones
	(Can't Get No) Satisfaction	The Rolling Stones
	Tears	Ken Dodd
	Help!	The Beatles
1966	*These Boots Are Made for Walkin'*	Nancy Sinatra
	Strangers in the Night	Frank Sinatra
	Green Green Grass of Home	Tom Jones
	The Sun Ain't Gonna Shine Anymore	The Walker Brothers
1967	*Release Me*	Engelbert Humperdinck
	A Whiter Shade of Pale	Procol Harum
	Puppet on a String	Sandie Shaw
	All You Need is Love	The Beatles
1968	*Congratulations*	Cliff Richard
	What a Wonderful World	Louis Armstrong
	Those Were the Days	Mary Hopkin
	Lily the Pink	Scaffold
1969	*Where Do You Go To, My Lovely?*	Peter Sarstedt
	Two Little Boys	Rolf Harris
	Something in the Air	Thunderclap Newman
	Sugar Sugar	The Archies
1970	*Bridge Over Troubled Water*	Simon and Garfunkel
	In the Summertime	Mungo Jerry
	All Kinds of everything	Dana
	The Wonder of You	Elvis Presley
1971	*My Sweet Lord*	George Harrison
	Grandad	Clive Dunn
	Ernie (the Fastest Milkman in the West)	Benny Hill
	Maggie May	Rod Stewart
1972	*I'd Like to Teach the World to Sing*	The New Seekers
	Puppy Love	Donny Osmond
	Mouldy Old Dough	Lieutenant Pigeon
	My Ding-A-Ling	Chuck Berry

1973	Blockbuster	Sweet
	Tie a Yellow Ribbon	Dawn
	Eye Level	Simon Park Orchestra
	Merry Xmas Everybody	Slade
1974	Waterloo	Abba
	Seasons in the Sun	Terry Jacks
	Tiger Feet	Mud
	She	Charles Aznavour
1975	Bohemian Rhapsody	Queen
	I'm Not in Love	10CC
	If	Telly Savalas
	Bye Bye Baby	The Bay City Rollers
1976	Mamma Mia	Abba
	Save Your Kisses for Me	Brotherhood of Man
	Dancing Queen	Abba
	Don't Go Breaking My Heart	Elton John and Kiki Dee
1977	Mull of Kintyre	Wings
	Don't Cry for Me, Argentina	Julie Covington
	Don't Give Up on Us	David Soul
	I Feel Love	Donna Summer
1978	Wuthering Heights	Kate Bush
	You're the One That I Want	John Travolta and
	Summer Nights	Olivia Newton John
	Three Times a Lady	Commodores
1979	Bright Eyes	Art Garfunkel
	Message in a Bottle	Police
	I Don't Like Mondays	Boomtown Rats
	Another Brick in the Wall	Pink Floyd
1980	Don't Stand So Close to Me	Police
	There's No One Quite Like	St Winifred's School
	Grandma	Choir
	Crying	Don McLean
	Woman in Love	Barbara Streisand

1981	*Imagine*	John Lennon
	Stand and Deliver	Adam and the Ants
	Don't You Want Me?	Human League
	Green Door	Shakin' Stevens

1982	*A Town Called Malice*	Jam
	Ebony and Ivory	Paul McCartney and Stevie Wonder
	Eye of the Tiger	Survivor
	Come on Eileen	Dexy's Midnight Runners

1983	*True*	Spandau Ballet
	Billie Jean	Michael Jackson
	Karma Chameleon	Culture Club
	Uptown Girl	Billy Joel

1984	*Do They Know it's Christmas*	Band Aid
	Pipes of Peace	Paul McCartney
	I Just Called to Say I Love You	Stevie Wonder
	Wake Me Up Before You Go-Go	Wham!

1985	*The Power of Love*	Jennifer Rush
	There Must Be An Angel	Eurythmics
	I Know Him So Well	Elaine Paige and Barbara Dickson
	A Good Heart	Feargal Sharkey

1986	*West End Girls*	Pet Shop Boys
	Living Doll	Cliff Richard and The Young Ones
	The Lady in Red	Chris De Burgh
	Take My Breath Away	Berlin

1987	*Never Gonna Give You Up*	Rick Astley
	Always on My Mind	Pet Shop Boys
	You Win Again	Bee Gees
	China in Your Hand	T'Pau

1988	*I Should Be So Lucky*	Kylie Minogue
	Orinoco Flow	Enya
	Mistletoe and Wine	Cliff Richard
	One Moment in Time	Whitney Houston
1989	*Eternal Flame*	Bangles
	Ferry 'Cross the Mersey	Gerry Marsden
	Belfast Child	Simple Minds
	Sealed With a Kiss	Jason Donovan
1990	*Unchained Melody*	Righteous Brothers
	A Little Time	Beautiful South
	Nothing Compares 2 U	Sinead O'Connor
	The Joker	Steve Miller Band
1991	*(Everything I Do) I Do It for You*	Bryan Adams
	Black or White	Michael Jackson
	Don't Let the Sun Go Down on Me	George Michael and Elton John
	Should I Stay or Should I Go	Clash
1992	*I Will Always Love You*	Whitney Houston
	Deeply Dippy	Right Said Fred
	Stay	Shakespears Sister
	Goodnight Girl	Wet Wet Wet
1993	*Young at Heart*	Bluebells
	Mr Vain	Culture Beat
	Babe	Take That
	Dreams	Gabrielle
1994	*Love Is All Around*	Wet Wet Wet
	Things Can Only Get Better	D:Ream
	Stay Another Day	East 17
	Without You	Mariah Carey
1995	*Think Twice*	Celine Dion
	Fairground	Simply Red
	Unchained Melody	Robson and Jerome
	Back for Good	Take That

1996	*Killing Me Softly*	Fugees
	Wannabe	Spice Girls
	How Deep is Your Love	Take That
	Jesus to a Child	George Michael
1997	*Candle in the Wind*	Elton John
	Perfect Day	Various Artists
	D'You Know What I Mean	Oasis
	Men in Black	Will Smith
1998	*Believe*	Cher
	Three Lions '98	Baddiel, Skinner and Lightning Seeds
	No Matter What	Boyzone
	Frozen	Madonna
1999	*When You Say Nothing At All*	Ronan Keating
	Millennium Prayer	Cliff Richard
	Mambo No 5	Lou Bega
	Livin' La Vida Loca	Ricky Martin
2000	*Rise*	Gabrielle
	Pure Shores	All Saints
	Against All Odds	Mariah Carey and Westlife
	Can We Fix It	Bob the Builder

Box Office Hits 1930–2000

1930 *All Quiet on the Western Front*
Animal Crackers
The Blue Angel
The Indians Are Coming

1931 *Mata Hari*
City Lights
Frankenstein
Cimarron

1932   *Tarzan the Ape Man*
Grand Hotel
Dr Jekyll and Mr Hyde
A Farewell to Arms

1933   *King Kong*
I'm No Angel
Duck Soup
Cavalcade

1934   *It Happened One Night*
Viva Villa!
The Man Who Knew Too Much
Bright Eyes

1935   *Mutiny on the Bounty*
Top Hat
A Night at the Opera
The Thirty-Nine Steps

1936   *The Great Ziegfeld*
Modern Times
The Charge of the Light Brigade
Follow the Fleet

1937   *A Day at the Races*
Snow White and the Seven Dwarfs
The Prisoner of Zenda
Oh, Mr Porter!

1938   *You Can't Take it with You*
Pygmalion
Boys Town
Jezebel

1939   *Gone with the Wind*
Goodbye, Mr Chips
The Wizard of Oz
Beau Geste

1940   *The Philadelphia Story*
In Which We Serve
Rebecca
Pinocchio

1941   *How Green Was My Valley*
Citizen Kane
Sergeant York
Dr Jekyll and Mr Hyde

1942   *Casablanca*
Mrs Miniver
In Which We Serve
Yankee Doodle Dandy

1943   *The Song of Bernadette*
For Whom the Bell Tolls
Heaven Can Wait
This is the Army

1944   *Going My Way*
This Happy Breed
Gaslight
Meet Me in St Louis

1945   *The Picture of Dorian Gray*
Brief Encounter
The Lost Weekend
The Wicked Lady

1946   *The Best Years of Our Lives*
To Each His Own
The Bells of St Mary's
The Road to Utopia

1947   *Gentleman's Agreement*
Brighton Rock
The Best Years of Our Lives
A Double Life

1948 *Hamlet*
Oliver Twist
The Road to Rio
The Red Shoes

1949 *The Third Man*
Kind Hearts and Coronets
All the King's Men
Joan of Arc

1950 *All About Eve*
Harvey
Annie Get Your Gun
Cinderella

1951 *A Streetcar Named Desire*
An American in Paris
Calamity Jane
The Lavender Hill Mob

1952 *The African Queen*
Singing in the Rain
High Noon
The Greatest Show on Earth

1953 *From Here To Eternity*
Roman Holiday
Gentlemen Prefer Blondes
The Robe

1954 *On the Waterfront*
White Christmas
Rear Window
The Dam Busters

1955 *To Catch a Thief*
Rebel Without a Cause
Blackboard Jungle
The Ladykillers

1956   *High Society*
The King and I
Around the World in Eighty Days
Trapeze

1957   *The Bridge on the River Kwai*
The Ten Commandments
Jailhouse Rock
Twelve Angry Men

1958   *Cat on a Hot Tin Roof*
South Pacific
Ice Cold in Alex
Vertigo

1959   *Ben Hur*
Some Like it Hot
Sleeping Beauty
North by Northwest

1960   *The Magnificent Seven*
Psycho
G.I. Blues
101 Dalmatians

1961   *West Side Story*
El Cid
Blue Hawaii
Breakfast at Tiffany's

1962   *Lawrence of Arabia*
To Kill a Mockingbird
Birdman of Alcatraz
Dr No

1963   *The Birds*
Tom Jones
Cleopatra
The Great Escape

1964 *My Fair Lady*
     Mary Poppins
     Goldfinger
     The Pink Panther

1965 *The Sound of Music*
     Dr Zhivago
     Cat Ballou
     The Magnificent Men in Their Flying Machines

1966 *A Man for All Seasons*
     Alfie
     Who's Afraid of Virginia Woolf?
     Our Man Flint

1967 *In the Heat of the Night*
     The Graduate
     Guess Who's Coming to Dinner
     The Jungle Book

1968 *Oliver!*
     Chitty Chitty Bang Bang
     Bullitt
     Funny Girl

1969 *True Grit*
     Butch Cassidy and the Sundance Kid
     Hello, Dolly!
     They Shoot Horses, Don't They?

1970 *Patton*
     The Railway Children
     Love Story
     Airport

1971 *The French Connection*
     A Clockwork Orange
     Klute
     Dirty Harry

1972   *The Godfather*
       Cabaret
       Last Tango in Paris
       Sleuth

1973   *The Sting*
       American Graffiti
       Jesus Christ Superstar
       Enter the Dragon

1974   *Murder on the Orient Express*
       The Man with the Golden Gun
       The Godfather, Part II
       The Towering Inferno

1975   *One Flew Over the Cuckoo's Nest*
       Jaws
       The Rocky Horror Picture Show
       Rollerball

1976   *Rocky*
       All the President's Men
       Marathon Man
       Bugsy Malone

1977   *Saturday Night Fever*
       Star Wars
       Annie Hall
       A Bridge Too Far

1978   *The Deer Hunter*
       Grease
       Superman
       Midnight Express

1979   *Kramer Versus Kramer*
       Apocalypse Now
       Monty Python's Life of Brian
       Escape from Alcatraz

1980 *Ordinary People*
      Raging Bull
      Coal Miner's Daughter
      The Elephant Man

1981 *Chariots of Fire*
      On Golden Pond
      Reds
      The French Lieutenant's Woman

1982 *Gandhi*
      Sophie's Choice
      Tootsie
      Blade Runner

1983 *Terms of Endearment*
      Tender Mercies
      Yentl
      Monty Python's The Meaning of Life

1984 *Amadeus*
      Places in the Heart
      The Killing Fields
      Greystoke: The Legend of Tarzan, Lord of the Apes

1985 *Out of Africa*
      Kiss of the Spider Woman
      Mask
      St Elmo's Fire

1986 *The Color of Money*
      Children of a Lesser God
      Platoon
      Hannah and Her Sisters

1987 *The Last Emperor*
      Wall Street
      Moonstruck
      The Living Daylights

1988 *Rain Man*
       The Accused
       A Fish Called Wanda
       Mississippi Burning

1989 *Driving Miss Daisy*
       My Left Foot
       Batman
       Dead Poets Society

1990 *Dances with Wolves*
       Misery
       Reversal of Fortune
       Dick Tracy

1991 *Silence of the Lambs*
       JFK
       Thelma and Louise
       Robin Hood; Prince of Thieves

1992 *Unforgiven*
       Howard's End
       Scent of a Woman
       The Bodyguard

1993 *Schindler's List*
       Philadelphia
       The Piano
       Jurassic Park

1994 *Forrest Gump*
       The Lion King
       Pulp Fiction
       True Lies

1995 *Braveheart*
       Dead Man Walking
       Apollo 13
       Golden Eye

1996 *The English Patient*
Independence Day
101 Dalmatians
Jerry Maguire

1997 *Titanic*
As Good as it Gets
Men in Black
Good Will Hunting

1998 *Saving Private Ryan*
Shakespeare in Love
There's Something about Mary
Patch Adams

1999 *American Beauty*
The Matrix
Runaway Bride
The World is not Enough

2000 *Gladiator*
Erin Brockovich
Billy Elliot
Charlie's Angels

Golden Years of Radio
Popular radio programmes 1930–1960

1930 First broadcast by The BBC Symphony Orchestra

1931 First broadcast by the BBC Theatre Orchestra

First broadcast by the BBC Chamber Orchestra

1932 Christmas Day broadcast by King George V

1933 *In Town Tonight*

1934 *Henry Hall's Guest Night*
In Your Garden
Coverage of the wedding of The Duke of Kent and Princess
Marina

1935 *The American Half Hour* with Alistair Cooke

1936 Death of King George V announced by John Reith
King Edward VIII's abdication broadcast

1937 *Farming Today*

1938 *Band Waggon*

1939 *ITMA (It's That Man Again)*
London Calling
Broadcast by Neville Chamberlain on the declaration of war

1940 Churchill's Prime Ministerial broadcasts
The Forces Programme
Music While You Work
Sunday Half Hour
Radio Newsreel

1941 *The Brains' Trust*
Workers' Playtime
Sincerely Yours

1942 *Desert Island Discs*
The Radio Doctor
The Man in Black

1943 *Saturday Night Theatre*
Yehudi Menuhin plays with the BBC Symphony Orchestra

1944 D-Day War Reports
Before the Ending of the Day

1945 VE-Day broadcasts by King George VI and Winston Churchill
VJ-Day broadcasts by King George VI and Clement Attlee
Family Favourites
Today in Parliament
Time for Verse

1946 *Housewives' Choice*
Woman's Hour
Dick Barton, Special Agent
Down Your Way
Letter from America

1947 *Much Binding in the Marsh*
Twenty Questions
Round Britain Quiz
How Does Your Garden Grow? (later renamed *Gardeners' Question Time*)

1948 *Take It From Here*
Mrs Dale's Diary
Top of the Form
Sports Report

1949 *A Book at Bedtime*
Morning Story
Billy Cotton's Band Show

1950 *Listen with Mother*
Life with the Lyons

1951 *The Archers*
Crazy People (to become *The Goons*)

1952 Funeral of King George VI

1953 *Friday Night is Music Night*
What Do You Know? (later renamed *Brain of Britain*)
The Glums

1954 *Hancock's Half Hour*
Any Answers?
Under Milk Wood

1955 *From Our Own Correspondent*
Pick of the Pops

1956 *My Word*

1957 The *Today* programme
Ball-by-ball cricket Test coverage (later renamed *Test Match Special*)
Record Review

1958 *Beyond Our Ken*

1959 *Sing Something Simple*
Your Hundred Best Tunes
Pick of the Week

Golden Years of Television
Popular television shows 1950–1980

1950   *Andy Pandy*
         Come Dancing

1951   *What's My Line?*

1952   Funeral of King George VI is televised
         Animal, Vegetable, Mineral
         Bill and Ben the Flowerpot Men
         Billy Bunter of Greyfriars School

1953   Coronation of Queen Elizabeth II
         Panorama
         The Good Old Days
         The Quatermass Experiment

1954   *Zoo Quest*
         The Grove Family
         Fabian of the Yard
         The Adventures of Rin Tin Tin

1955   *This is Your Life*
         Dixon of Dock Green
         Life with the Lyons
         The Brains Trust

1956   *Hancock's Half Hour*
         Opportunity Knocks
         Billy Cotton Band Show
         Father Knows Best

1957   *Alfred Hitchcock Presents*
         The Army Game
         6.5 Special
         Emergency Ward 10

1958 *Blue Peter*
Grandstand
Cheyenne
The Black and White Minstrel Show

1959 *Juke Box Jury*
Face to Face
Pick of the Week
Whicker's World

1960 *Coronation Street*
Danger Man
Bonanza
Candid Camera

1961 *The Avengers*
Songs of Praise
Dr Kildare
The Rag Trade

1962 *Z-Cars*
The Saint
Dr Finlay's Casebook
That Was the Week that Was

1963 *Doctor Who*
Ready Steady Go
The Fugitive
The Andy Williams Show

1964 *Top of the Pops*
Crossroads
The Great War
Match of the Day

1965 *World of Sport*
Not Only… But Also
Tomorrow's World
The Likely Lads

1966   *Softly Softly*
        Till Death Us Do Part
        It's a Knockout
        The Frost Report

1967   *The Forsyte Saga*
        The Prisoner
        Face the Music
        The Golden Shot

1968   *Dad's Army*
        Magpie
        Father Dear Father
        Sportsnight with Coleman

1969   *Monty Python's Flying Circus*
        The Liver Birds
        Pot Black
        Live transmission of the Moon landing

1970   *Play for Today*
        Doomwatch
        UFO
        Up Pompeii!

1971   *Bruce Forsyth and The Generation Game*
        The Two Ronnies
        Sale of the Century
        The Onedin Line

1972   *Emmerdale Farm*
        Mastermind
        War and Peace
        Mr and Mrs

1973   *Superstars*
        New Faces
        Man About the House
        That's Life

1974 *The Waltons*
Little House on the Prairie
Porridge
It Ain't Half Hot Mum

1975 *The Sweeney*
The Good Life
Jim'll Fix It
Fawlty Towers

1976 *When the Boat Comes In*
I, Claudius
The Duchess of Duke Street
Poldark

1977 *Roots*
Charlie's Angels
Blankety Blank
The Professionals

1978 *All Creatures Great and Small*
Dallas
Butterflies
3-2-1

1979 *Question Time*
Antiques Road Show
Tinker, Tailor, Soldier, Spy
To the Manor Born

1980 *Newsnight*
Yes, Minister
Juliet Bravo
Campion

Books of the Year 1930 - 2000

1930 *Angel Pavement* – J.B. Priestly
Exile – Warwick Deeping
Cimarron – Edna Ferber
Rogue Herries – Hugh Walpole

1931 *A White Bird Flying* – Bess Streeter Aldrich
The Bridge of Desire – Warwick Deeping
The Good Earth – Pearl S. Buck
Shadows on the Rock – Willa Cather

1932 *Brave New World* – Aldous Huxley
Stamboul Train – Graham Greene
Black Mischief – Evelyn Waugh
The Fountain – Charles Morgan

1933 *One More River* – John Galsworthy
Forgive Us Our Trespassers – Lloyd C. Douglas
As the Earth Turns – Gladys Hasty Carroll
Anthony Adverse – Hervey Allen

1934 *Lamb in His Bosom* – Caroline Miller
So Red the Rose – Stark Young
Good-Bye, Mr Chips – James Hilton
Work of Art – Sinclair Lewis

1935 *Green Light* – Lloyd C. Douglas
Vein of Iron – Ellen Glasgow
Lost Horizon – James Hilton
Heaven's My Destination – Thornton Wilder

1936 *Gone with the Wind* – Margaret Mitchell
Eyeless in Gaza – Aldous Huxley
The Last Puritan – George Santayana
Sparkenbroke – Charles Morgan

1937 *Of Mice and Men* – John Steinbeck
Theatre – W. Somerset Maugham
The Citadel – A.J. Cronin
The Rains Came – Louis Bromfield

1938 *Rebecca* – Daphne du Maurier
The Yearling – Marjorie Kinnan Rawlings
My Son, My Son! – Howard Spring
Northwest Passage – Kenneth Roberts

1939 *The Grapes of Wrath* – John Steinbeck
Wickford Point – John P. Marquand
Escape – Ethel Vance
Disputed Passage – Lloyd C. Douglas

1940 *How Green Was My Valley* – Richard Llewellyn
Mrs Miniver – Jan Struther
For Whom the Bell Tolls – Ernest Hemingway
Night in Bombay – Louis Bromfield

1941 *Random Harvest* – James Hilton
This Above All – Eric Knight
The Keys of the Kingdom – A.J. Cronin
The Sun is My Undoing – Marguerite Steen

1942 *The Song of Bernadette* – Franz Werfel
The Moon is Down – John Steinbeck
The Robe – Lloyd C. Douglas
Dragon Seed – Pearl S. Buck

1943 *The Valley of Decision* – Marcia Davenport
So Little Time – John P. Marquand
Mrs Parkington – Louis Bromfield
A Tree Grows in Brooklyn – Betty Smith

1944 *Strange Fruit* – Lillian Smith
The Razor's Edge – W. Somerset Maugham
Forever Amber – Kathleen Winsor
The Green Years – A.J. Cronin

1945 *The Black Rose* – Thomas B. Costain
The White Tower – James Ramsay Ullman
Cass Timberlane – Sinclair Lewis
So Well Remembered – James Hilton

1946 *The King's General* – Daphne du Maurier
The River Road – Frances Parkinson Keyes
The Hucksters – Frederic Wakeman
This Side of Innocence – Taylor Caldwell

1947 *The Miracle of the Bells* – Russell Janney
The Money Man – Thomas B. Costain
The Wayward Bus – John Steinbeck
East Side, West Side – Marcia Davenport

1948 *Tomorrow Will Be Better* – Betty Smith
Dinner at Antoine's – Frances Parkinson Keyes
The Naked and the Dead – Norman Mailer
The Bishop's Mantle – Agnes Sligh Turnbull

1949 *The Big Fisherman* – Lloyd C. Douglas
The Egyptian – Mika Waltari
Mary – Sholem Asch
Point of No Return – John P. Marquand

1950 *The Parasites* – Daphne du Maurier
Across the River and into the Trees – Ernest Hemingway
The Cardinal – Henry Morton Robinson
The Wall – John Hersey

1951 *The Cruel Sea* – Nicholas Montsarrat
The Caine Mutiny – Herman Wouk
From Here to Eternity – James Jones
A Woman Called Fancy – Frank Yerby

1952 *East of Eden* – John Steinbeck
The Old Man and the Sea – Ernest Hemingway
The Silver Chalice – Thomas B. Costain
My Cousin Rachel – Daphne du Maurier

1953 *Desiree* – Annemarie Selinko
Battle Cry – Leon Uris
The High and the Mighty – Ernest K. Gann
Beyond This Place – A.J. Cronin

1954   *Lord of the Flies* – William Golding
  Lucky Jim – Kingsley Amis
  Mary Anne – Daphne du Maurier
  Love is Eternal – Irving Stone

1955   *Moonraker* – Ian Fleming
  Lolita – Vladimir Nabokov
  Marjorie Morningstar – Herman Wouk
  Andersonville – MacKinlay Kantor

1956   *Peyton Place* – Grace Metalious
  Don't Go Near the Water – William Brinkley
  The Last Hurrah – Edwin O'Connor
  Eloise – Kay Thompson

1957   *On the Beach* – Nevil Shute
  The Scapegoat – Daphne du Maurier
  Compulsion – Meyer Levin
  By Love Possessed – James Gould Cozzens

1958   *Doctor Zhivago* – Boris Pasternak
  From the Terrace – John O'Hara
  Ice Palace – Edna Ferber
  Victorine – Frances Parkinson Keyes

1959   *Exodus* – Leon Uris
  Lady Chatterley's Lover – D.H. Lawrence
  The Ugly American – Eugene L. Burdick
  Advise and Consent – Allen Drury

1960   *Trustee from the Toolroom* – Nevil Shute
  The Chapman Report – Irving Wallace
  Ourselves to Know – John O'Hara
  The Constant Image – Marcia Davenport

1961   *To Kill a Mockingbird* – Harper Lee
  The Carpetbaggers – Harold Robbins
  The Winter of Our Discontent – John Steinbeck
  The Agony and the Ecstasy – Irving Stone

1962   *Youngblood Hawk* – Herman Wouk
The Prize – Irving Wallace
Ship of Fools – Katherine Anne Porter
Dearly Beloved – Anne Morrow Lindbergh

1963   *Caravans* – James A. Michener
The Glass Blowers – Daphne du Maurier
The Shoes of the Fisherman – Morris L. West
The Group – Mary McCarthy

1964   *The Spy Who Came in from the Cold* – John Le Carré
You Only Live Twice – Ian Fleming
Armageddon – Leon Uris
The Man – Irving Wallace

1965   *Hotel* – Arthur Hailey
Up the Down Staircase – Bel Kaufman
The Source – James A. Michener
Herzog – Saul Bellow

1966   *Valley of the Dolls* – Jacqueline Susann
The Adventurers – Harold Robbins
The Double Image – Helen MacInnes
The Fixer – Bernard Malamud

1967   *Rosemary's Baby* – Ira Levin
The Plot – Irving Wallace
Topaz – Leon Uris
Christy – Catherine Marshall

1968   *Airport* – Arthur Hailey
Couples – John Updike
Testimony of Two Men – Taylor Caldwell
A Small Town in Germany – John Le Carré

1969   *The Godfather* – Mario Puzo
The Andromeda Strain – Michael Crichton
The Inheritors – Harold Robbins
The Love Machine – Jacqueline Susann

1970   *The French Lieutenant's Woman* – John Fowles
Love Story – Erich Segal
Islands in the Stream – Ernest Hemingway
Travels with My Aunt – Graham Greene

1971   *The Day of the Jackal* – Frederick Forsyth
The Betsy – Harold Robbins
Wheels – Arthur Hailey
The Winds of War – Herman Wouk

1972   *Jonathan Livingston Seagull* – Richard Bach
The Odessa File – Frederick Forsyth
August, 1914 – Alexander Solzhenitsyn
The Word – Irving Wallace

1973   *The Honorary Consul* – Graham Greene
Once is Not Enough – Jacqueline Susann
Breakfast of Champions – Kurt Vonnegut
Burr – Gore Vidal

1974   *Watership Down* – Richard Adams
Tinker, Tailor, Soldier, Spy – John Le Carré
Jaws – Peter Benchley
The Dogs of War – Frederick Forsyth

1975   *The Eagle Has Landed* – Jack Higgins
The Great Train Robbery – Michael Crichton
The Moneychangers – Arthur Hailey
Shogun – James Clavell

1976   *The Deep* – Peter Benchley
Sleeping Murder – Agatha Christie
Trinity – Leon Uris
Dolores – Jacqueline Susann

1977   *The Thorn Birds* – Colleen McCullough
The Silmarillion – J.R.R. Tolkien and Christopher Tolkien
Beggarman, Thief – Irwin Shaw
Dreams Die First – Harold Robbins

1978 *War and Remembrance* – Herman Wouk
      Chesapeake – James A. Michener
      The Holcroft Covenant – Robert Ludlum
      Fools Die – Mario Puzo

1979 *Sophie's Choice* – William Styron
      The Dead Zone – Stephen King
      Smiley's People – John Le Carré
      Overload – Arthur Hailey

1980 *The Bourne Identity* – Robert Ludlum
      The Covenant – James A. Michener
      The Key to Rebecca – Ken Follett
      Rage of Angels – Sidney Sheldon

1981 *Midnight's Children* – Salman Rushdie
      Silver's City – Maurice Leitch
      Gorky Park – Martin Cruz Smith
      Noble House – James Clavell

1982 *Schindler's Ark* – Thomas Keneally
      2010: Odyssey Two – Arthur C. Clarke
      E.T., The Extra-terrestrial – William Kotzwinkle
      Young Shoulders – John Wain

1983 *Return of the Jedi* – Joan D. Vinge
      The Color Purple – Alice Walker
      The Little Drummer Girl – John Le Carré
      Fools of Fortune – William Trevor

1984 *Hotel du Lac* – Anita Brookner
      Kruger's Alp – Christopher Hope
      The Sicilian – Mario Puzo
      The Fourth Protocol – Frederick Forsyth

1985 *Foreign Affairs* – Alison Lurie
      The Bone People – Keri Hulme
      Hawksmoor – Peter Ackroyd
      Lake Wobegon Days – Garrison Keillor

1986   *An Artist of the Floating World* – Kazuo Ishiguro
       The Old Devils – Kingsley Amis
       Lonesome Dove – Larry McMurty
       A Perfect Spy – John Le Carré

1987   *Spycatcher* – Peter Wright
       Moon Tiger – Penelope Lively
       A Child in Time – Ian McEwan
       Patriot Games – Tom Clancy

1988   *Oscar and Lucinda* – Peter Carey
       Beloved – Toni Morrison
       The Satanic Verses – Salman Rushdie
       A Brief History of Time – Stephen Hawking

1989   *The Remains of the Day* – Kazuo Ishiguro
       Breathing Lessons – Anne Tyler
       London Fields – Martin Amis
       The Russia House – John Le Carré

1990   *Hopeful Monsters* – Nicholas Mosley
       Possession – A.S. Byatt
       The Bourne Ultimatum – Robert Ludlum
       Jurassic Park – Michael Crichton

1991   *The Famished Road* – Ben Okri
       Rabbit at Rest – John Updike
       A Thousand Acres – Jane Smiley
       The Firm – John Grisham

1992   *Paddy Clarke Ha Ha Ha* – Roddy Doyle
       Men are from Mars, Women are from Venus – John Gray
       The English Patient – Michael Ondaatje
       The Pelican Brief – John Grisham

1993   *Theory of War* – Joan Brady
       The Bridges of Madison County – Robert James Waller
       The Client – John Grisham
       Honour Among Thieves – Jeffrey Archer

1994   *The Shipping News* – E Annie Prouix
How Late it Was, How Late – James Kelman
Felicia's Journey – William Trevor
Disclosure – Michael Crichton

1995   *The Stone Diaries* – Carol Shields
The Moor's Last Sigh – Salman Rushdie
The Ghost Road – Pat Barker
The Horse Whisperer – Nicholas Evans

1996   *Independence Day* – Richard Ford
Every Man for Himself – Beryl Bainbridge
Last Orders – Graham Swift
The Fourth Estate – Jeffrey Archer

1997   *The God of Small Things* – Arundhati Roy
Harry Potter and the Philosopher's Stone – J.K. Rowling
The Partner – John Grisham
Cold Mountain – Charles Frazier

1998   *American Pastoral* – Philip Roth
Harry Potter and the Chamber of Secrets – J.K. Rowling
About a Boy – Nick Hornby
Amsterdam – Ian McEwan

1999   *Harry Potter and the Prisoner of Azkaban* – J.K. Rowling
The Hours – Michael Cunningham
Charlotte Gray – Sebastian Faulks
Disgrace – J.M. Coetzee

2000   *Harry Potter and the Goblet of Fire* – J.K. Rowling
When I Lived in Modern Times – Linda Grant
The Blind Assassin – Margaret Atwood
The Amber Spyglass – Philip Pullman

Deaths 1930 – 2000
British unless specified otherwise

1930   Lord Balfour – Prime Minister
Robert Bridges – Poet Laureate
Sir Henry Seagrave – holder of world speedboat record
Sir Arthur Conan Doyle – creator of Sherlock Holmes

1931   Anna Pavlova – Russian ballerina
Dame Nellie Melba – Australian soprano
Jesse Boot (Lord Trent) – founder of Boots the Chemist
Thomas Edison – American inventor and scientist

1932   C.P. Scott – editor of *The (Manchester) Guardian*
Edgar Wallace – author
Charles Lindbergh Jnr – (kidnapped American baby)
Rin Tin Tin – canine movie star

1933   Calvin Coolidge – 30th American President
John Galsworthy – author
Sir Frederick Henry Royce – car builder
Jack Pickford – American actor

1934   Sir Edward Elgar – composer
Gustav Holst – composer
Frederick Delius – composer
Field Marshal Paul von Hindenburg – German President

1935   Colonel T.E. Lawrence 'of Arabia' – soldier and writer
Max Liebermann – German painter
Earl John Rushworth Jellicoe – Admiral of the Fleet in
World War I
Will Rogers – American actor

1936   King George V
Rudyard Kipling – poet and author
G.K. Chesterton – author
Louis Bleriot – French aviator

1937   Harry Vardon – golfer
Jean Harlow – American actress
George Gershwin – American composer
James Ramsay MacDonald – first Labour Prime Minister

1938   Joe 'King' Oliver – American jazz musician
Mustapha Kemal Ataturk – Turkish statesman
Pearl White – American silent actress
Florence Lawrence – American actress

1939   W.B. Yeats – Irish poet and playwright
Pope Pius XI
Sigmund Freud – Austrian psychoanalyst
Douglas Fairbanks – American actor

1940   John Buchan, Lord Tweedsmuir – author and politician
Leon Trotsky – Soviet Socialist statesman and writer
Neville Chamberlain – Prime Minister
F. Scott Fitzgerald – American author

1941   Amy Johnson – aviator
Lord Robert Baden-Powell – founder of the Boy Scouts
James Joyce – Irish author
Virginia Woolf – author

1942   Reinhard Heydrich – Nazi architect of the 'Final Solution'
The Duke of Kent
John Barrymore – American actor
Carole Lombard – American actress

1943   Leslie Howard – actor
General Wladislaw Sikorski – Polish Commander-in-Chief
Jean Moulin ('Max') – French Resistance leader
Beatrix Potter – author

1944   Major General Orde Charles Wingate – military commander
Sir Henry Wood – conductor
Erwin Rommel – German Field Marshal
Glen Miller – American bandleader

1945 Adolf Hitler – German dictator
David Lloyd George – Prime Minister
Benito Mussolini – Italian dictator
Franklin D. Roosevelt – American President

1946 John Logie Baird – television pioneer
H.G. Wells – author
Hermann Goering – German Nazi
W.C. Fields – American actor

1947 Al Capone – American gangster
Henry Ford – American car maker
Stanley Baldwin – Prime Minister
Adrienne Ames – American actress

1948 Mahatma Gandhi – Indian leader
Orville Wright – American aviator
George Herman 'Babe' Ruth – American baseball player
Carole Landis – American actress

1949 Tommy Handley – comedian
Margaret Mitchell – American author
Fritz Hart – composer
Richard Strauss – German composer

1950 George Orwell – author
Sir Harry Lauder – Scottish comedian
Jan Smuts – South African statesman
George Bernard Shaw – Irish playwright

1951 Ivor Novello – actor and composer
Ernest Bevin – politician
William Randolph Hearst – American press magnate
Lloyd C. Douglas – American author

1952 George VI
Sir Stafford Cripps – politician
Eva Peron – Argentinian politician
Viscount Waldorf Astor – American-born politician

1953   Josef Stalin – Soviet leader
Kathleen Ferrier – opera singer
Dylan Thomas – poet
Queen Mary – widow of George VI

1954   Sir George Robey – comedian
Lionel Barrymore – actor
Henri Matisse – French artist
Alan Turing – mathematician and code-breaker

1955   Sir Alexander Fleming – biologist
James Dean – American actor
Albert Einstein – German-born American scientist

1956   A.A. Milne – author
C.B. Fry – cricketer
Tommy Dorsey – American musician
Bertolt Brecht – German playwright

1957   Humphrey Bogart – American actor
Oliver Hardy – American comedian
Dorothy Sayers – author
Joseph McCarthy – American senator

1958   Pope Pius XII
Ronald Colman – actor
Douglas Jardine – cricketer
Christabel Pankhurst – Suffragette

1959   Mike Hawthorn – racing driver
Buddy Holly – American rock singer
Billie Holliday – American blues singer
Errol Flynn – actor

1960   Nevil Shute – author
Aneurin Bevan – politician
Clark Gable – American actor
Albert Camus – French writer

1961   George Formby – comedian
Sir Thomas Beecham – conductor
Gary Cooper – American actor
Ernest Hemingway – American author

1962   Marilyn Monroe – American actress
Charles Laughton – actor
Adolf Eichmann – German Nazi
Eleanor Roosevelt – American First Lady

1963   John F. Kennedy – American President
Hugh Gaitskell – politician
Pope John XXIII
Edith Piaf – French singer

1964   Jawaharlal Nehru – Indian leader
Ian Fleming – author
Cole Porter – American composer
Jim Reeves – American singer

1965   Winston Churchill – Prime Minister
Nat King Cole – American singer
Richard Dimbleby – broadcaster
W. Somerset Maugham – author

1966   Walt Disney – American animator
Buster Keaton – American actor
Evelyn Waugh – author
Montgomery Clift – American actor

1967   Donald Campbell – speedster on land and water
Clement Attlee – Prime Minister
Spencer Tracy – American actor
Jayne Mansfield – American actress

1968   Dr Martin Luther King – American civil rights leader
Jim Clark – racing driver
Bobby Kennedy – American politican
Tony Hancock – comedian

1969   Richmal Crompton – author
        General Dwight Eisenhower – American President
        Rocky Marciano – American boxer
        Brian Jones – guitarist with the Rolling Stones

1970   Bertrand Russell – philosopher
        Jimi Hendrix – American musician
        Janis Joplin – American singer
        General Charles de Gaulle – French President

1971   Sonny Liston – American boxer
        Nikita Khrushchev – Soviet leader
        Louis Armstrong – American jazz singer and trumpeter
        'Papa Doc' Duvalier – Haitian dictator

1972   Cecil Day Lewis – Poet Laureate
        Duke of Windsor – ex-King Edward VIII
        Harry S. Truman – American President
        Dame Margaret Rutherford – actress

1973   Lyndon Baines Johnson – American President
        Sir Noel Coward – playwright
        Betty Grable – American actress
        W.H. Auden – poet

1974   Duke Ellington – American jazz musician
        Juan Peron – Argentinian President
        Georges Pompidou – French President
        Bud Abbott – American actor

1975   Graham Hill – racing driver
        General Francisco Franco – Spanish leader
        Dame Barbara Hepworth – sculptor
        Eamon de Valera – Irish Premier

1976   Dame Agatha Christie – author
        Field Marshal Bernard Montgomery – World War II commander
        Mao Tse-tung – Chinese leader
        Benjamin Britten – composer

1977 Anthony Eden – Prime Minister
Elvis Presley – American rock singer
Bing Crosby – American singer and actor
Marc Bolan – rock singer

1978 Pope Paul VI
Pope John-Paul
Jomo Kenyatta – Kenyan leader
Golda Meir – Israeli leader

1979 Airey Neave – politician
John Wayne – American actor
Lord Louis Mountbatten – commander and statesman
Dame Gracie Fields – singer and actress

1980 John Lennon – musician and 'Beatle'
Peter Sellers – actor and comedian
Steve McQueen – American actor
Sir Alfred Hitchock – film director

1981 Bill Haley – American rock singer
Mike Hailwood – motorcyclist
Bob Marley – Jamaican reggae singer
Anwar Sadat – Egyptian President

1982 Henry Fonda – American actor
Ingrid Bergman – American actress
Princess Grace of Monaco – former American actress
Leonid Brezhnev – Soviet President

1983 William Walton – composer
David Niven – actor
Sir Ralph Richardson – actor
Tennessee Williams – American playwright

1984 Eric Morecambe – comedian
Marvin Gaye – American singer
Indira Gandhi – Indian Prime Minister
Richard Burton – actor

1985 Sir Michael Redgrave – actor
Laura Ashley – designer and entrepreneur
Rock Hudson – American actor
Orson Welles – American actor and director

1986 James Cagney – American actor
Jim Laker – cricketer
Harold Macmillan – Prime Minister
Cary Grant – British-born American actor

1987 Andy Warhol – American artist
Danny Kaye – American actor
Fred Astaire – Amercian actor and dancer
Eamonn Andrews – broadcaster

1988 Trevor Howard – actor
Roy Orbison – American singer
Kim Philby – spy
Andy Gibb – Australian singer

1989 Lord Laurence Olivier – actor
Salvador Dali – Spanish artist
Bette Davis – American actress
Anthony Quayle – actor

1990 Len Hutton – cricketer
Roald Dahl – author
Sammy Davis Jr – American entertainer
Greta Garbo – Swedish actress

1991 Dame Peggy Ashcroft – actress
Graham Greene – author
Lee Remick – American actress
Michael Landon – American actor

1992 Freddie Mercury – Zanzibar-born singer
Marlene Dietrich – German actress
Denholm Elliott – actor
Benny Hill – comedian

1993   Bobby Moore – footballer
Stewart Grainger – American actor
Arthur Ashe – American tennis player
Vincent Price – actor

1994   John Smith – Leader of the Labour Party
Ayrton Senna – Brazilian racing driver
Burt Lancaster – American actor
Henry Mancini – composer

1995   Donald Pleasance – actor
Ginger Rogers – American actress/dancer
Dean Martin – American singer/actor
Peter Cook – satirist

1996   Gene Kelly – American actor/dancer
Greer Garson – actress
Jon Pertwee – actor
Willie Rushton – satirist

1997   Diana, Princess of Wales
Mother Teresa – Albanian missionary
Robert Mitchum – American actor
James Stewart – American actor

1998   Frank Sinatra – American singer/actor
Tammy Wynette – American singer
Dame Catherine Cookson – author
Frank Muir – comedy writer

1999   Oliver Reed – actor
Jill Dando – journalist and TV presenter
Dirk Bogarde – actor
Iris Murdoch – author

2000   Sir Alec Guinness – actor
Sir John Gielgud – actor
Sir Stanley Matthews – footballer
Ian Dury – singer

English Football League and FA Cup Winners 1930–2000

	League	FA Cup
1930	Sheffield Wednesday	Arsenal 2-0 Huddersfield Town
1931	Arsenal	West Bromwich Albion 2-1 Birmingham City
1932	Everton	Newcastle United 2-1 Arsenal
1933	Arsenal	Everton 3-0 Manchester City
1934	Arsenal	Manchester City 2-1 Portsmouth
1935	Arsenal	Sheffield Wednesday 4-2 West Bromwich Albion
1936	Sunderland	Arsenal 1-0 Sheffield United
1937	Manchester City	Sunderland 3-1 Preston North End
1938	Arsenal	Preston North End 1-0 Huddersfield Town
1939	Everton	Portsmouth 4-1 Wolverhampton Wanderers
1940	*Not held*	*Not held*
1941	*Not held*	*Not held*
1942	*Not held*	*Not held*
1943	*Not held*	*Not held*
1944	*Not held*	*Not held*
1945	*Not held*	*Not held*
1946	*Not held*	Derby County 4-1 Charlton Athletic
1947	Liverpool	Charlton Athletic 1-0 Burnley
1948	Arsenal	Manchester United 4-2 Blackpool
1949	Portsmouth	Wolverhampton Wanderers 3-1 Leicester City
1950	Portsmouth	Arsenal 2-0 Liverpool
1951	Tottenham Hotspur	Newcastle United 2-0 Blackpool
1952	Manchester United	Newcastle United 1-0 Arsenal
1953	Arsenal	Blackpool 4-3 Bolton Wanderers
1954	Wolverhampton Wanderers	West Bromwich Albion 3-2 Preston North End
1955	Chelsea	Newcastle United 3-1 Manchester City
1956	Manchester United	Manchester City 3-1 Birmingham City
1957	Manchester United	Aston Villa 2-1 Manchester United
1958	Wolverhampton Wanderers	Bolton Wanderers 2-0 Manchester United
1959	Wolverhampton Wanderers	Nottingham Forest 2-1 Luton Town

	League	FA Cup
1960	Burnley	Wolverhampton Wanderers 3-0 Blackburn Rovers
1961	Tottenham Hotspur	Tottenham Hotspur 2-0 Leicester City
1962	Ipswich Town	Tottenham Hotspur 3-1 Burnley
1963	Everton	Manchester United 3-1 Leicester City
1964	Liverpool	West Ham United 3-2 Preston North End
1965	Manchester United	Liverpool 2-1 Leeds United
1966	Liverpool	Everton 3-2 Sheffield Wednesday
1967	Manchester United	Tottenham Hotspur 2-1 Chelsea
1968	Manchester City	West Bromwich Albion 1-0 Everton
1969	Leeds United	Manchester City 1-0 Leicester City
1970	Everton	Chelsea 2-1 Leeds United*
1971	Arsenal	Arsenal 2-1 Liverpool
1972	Derby County	Leeds United 1-0 Arsenal
1973	Liverpool	Sunderland 1-0 Leeds United
1974	Leeds United	Liverpool 3-0 Newcastle United
1975	Derby County	West Ham United 2-0 Fulham
1976	Liverpool	Southampton 1-0 Manchester United
1977	Liverpool	Manchester United 2-1 Liverpool
1978	Nottingham Forest	Ipswich Town 1-0 Arsenal
1979	Liverpool	Arsenal 3-2 Manchester United
1980	Liverpool	West Ham United 1-0 Arsenal
1981	Aston Villa	Tottenham Hotspur 3-2 Manchester City*
1982	Liverpool	Tottenham Hotspur 1-0 Queen's Park Rangers*
1983	Liverpool	Manchester United 4-0 Brighton & Hove Albion*
1984	Liverpool	Everton 2-0 Watford
1985	Everton	Manchester United 1-0 Everton
1986	Liverpool	Liverpool 3-1 Everton
1987	Everton	Coventry City 3-2 Tottenham Hotspur
1988	Liverpool	Wimbledon 1-0 Liverpool
1989	Arsenal	Liverpool 3-2 Everton
1990	Liverpool	Manchester United 1-0 Crystal Palace*
1991	Arsenal	Tottenham Hotspur 2-1 Nottingham Forest
1992	Leeds United	Liverpool 2-0 Sunderland

Premier League

1993	Manchester United	Arsenal 2-1 Sheffield Wednesday
1994	Manchester United	Manchester United 4-0 Chelsea
1995	Blackburn Rovers	Everton 1-0 Manchester United
1996	Manchester United	Manchester United 1-0 Liverpool
1997	Manchester United	Chelsea 2-0 Middlesbrough
1998	Arsenal	Arsenal 2-0 Newcastle United
1999	Manchester United	Manchester United 2-0 Newcastle United
2000	Manchester United	Chelsea 1-0 Aston Villa

* Replay

Football World Cup Winners

Year	Venue	Final		
1930	Uruguay	Uruguay	4-2	Argentina
1934	Italy	Italy	2-1	Czechoslovakia
1938	France	Italy	4-2	Hungary
1950	Brazil	Uruguay	2-1	Brazil
1954	Switzerland	West Germany	3-2	Hungary
1958	Sweden	Brazil	5-2	Sweden
1962	Chile	Brazil	3-1	Czechoslovakia
1966	England	England	4-2	West Germany
1970	Mexico	Brazil	4-1	Italy
1974	West Germany	West Germany	2-1	Holland
1978	Argentina	Argentina	3-1	Holland
1982	Spain	Italy	3-1	West Germany
1986	Mexico	Argentina	3-2	West Germany
1990	Italy	West Germany	1-0	Argentina
1994	USA	Brazil	0-0	Italy (penalties Brazil 3-2)
1998	France	France	3-0	Brazil
2002	Japan	Brazil	2-0	Germany
2006	Germany	Italy	1-1	France (penalties Italy 5-3)

Cricket County Champions 1930–2000

1930	Lancashire	1969	Glamorgan
1931	Yorkshire	1970	Kent
1932	Yorkshire	1971	Surrey
1933	Yorkshire	1972	Warwickshire
1934	Lancashire	1973	Hampshire
1935	Yorkshire	1974	Worcestershire
1936	Derbyshire	1975	Leicestershire
1937	Yorkshire	1976	Middlesex
1938	Yorkshire	1977	Kent/Middlesex
1939	Yorkshire	1978	Kent
1946	Yorkshire	1979	Essex
1947	Middlesex	1980	Middlesex
1948	Glamorgan	1981	Nottinghamshire
1949	Middlesex/Yorkshire	1982	Middlesex
1950	Lancashire/Surrey	1983	Essex
1951	Warwickshire	1984	Essex
1952	Surrey	1985	Middlesex
1953	Surrey	1986	Essex
1954	Surrey	1987	Nottinghamshire
1955	Surrey	1988	Worcestershire
1956	Surrey	1989	Worcestershire
1957	Surrey	1990	Middlesex
1958	Surrey	1991	Essex
1959	Yorkshire	1992	Essex
1960	Yorkshire	1993	Middlesex
1961	Hampshire	1994	Warwickshire
1962	Yorkshire	1995	Warwickshire
1963	Yorkshire	1996	Leicestershire
1964	Worcestershire	1997	Glamorgan
1965	Worcestershire	1998	Leicestershire
1966	Yorkshire	1999	Surrey
1967	Yorkshire	2000	Surrey
1968	Yorkshire		

Horse Racing

The Grand National and Derby Winners 1930–2000

	The Derby		The Grand National	
	Horse	*Jockey*	*Horse*	*Jockey*
1930	Blenheim	H Wragg	Shaun Goilin	T Cullinan
1931	Cameronian	F Fox	Grakle	R Lyall
1932	April the Fifth	F Lane	Forbra	J Hamey
1933	Hyperion	T Weston	Kellsboro Jack	D Williams
1934	Windsor Lad	C Smirke	Golden Miller	G Wilson
1935	Bahram	F Fox	Reynoldstown	FC Furlong
1936	Mahmoud	C Smirke	Reynoldstown	FT Walwyn
1937	Mid-day Sun	M Beary	Royal Mail	E Williams
1938	Bois Roussel	C Elliot	Battleship	B Hobbs
1939	Blue Peter	E Smith	Workman	T Hyde
1940	Pont L'Eveque	S Wragg	Bogskar	M Jones
1941	Owen Tudor	W Nevett	*No race*	-
1942	Watling Street	H Wragg	*No race*	-
1943	Straight Deal	T Carey	*No race*	-
1944	Ocean Swell	W Nevett	*No race*	-
1945	Dante	W Nevett	*No race*	-
1946	Airborne	T Lowrey	Lovely Cottage	Capt R Petre
1947	Pearl Diver	G Brigland	Caughoo	E Dempsey
1948	My Love	W Johnstone	Sheila's Cottage	AP Thompson
1949	Nimbus	C Elliot	Russian Hero	L McMorrow
1950	Galcador	WR Johnstone	Freebooter	J Power
1951	Arctic Prince	C Spares	Nickel Coin	JA Bullock
1952	Tulyar	C Smirke	Teal	AP Thompson
1953	Pinza	G Richards	Early Mist	B Marshall
1954	Never Say Die	L Piggott	Royal Tan	B Marshall
1955	Phil Drake	F Palmer	Quare Times	P Taaffe
1956	Lavandin	WR Johnstone	E.S.B.	DV Dick
1957	Crepello	L Piggott	Sundew	F Winter
1958	Hard Ridden	C Smirke	Mr What	AR Freeman
1959	Parthia	W Carr	Oxo	M Scudamore
1960	St Paddy	L Piggott	Merryman II	G Scott
1961	Psidium	R Poincelet	Nicolaus Silver	R Beasley
1962	Larkspur	N Sellwood	Kilmore	F Winter
1963	Relko	Y Saint-Martin	Ayala	P Buckley
1964	Santa Claus	A Breasley	Team Spirit	W Robinson

	The Derby		**The Grand National**	
	Horse	*Jockey*	*Horse*	*Jockey*
1965	Sea Bird II	TP Glennon	Jay Trump	T Smith
1966	Charlottown	A Breasley	Anglo	T Norman
1967	Royal Place	G Moore	Foinavon	J Buckingham
1968	Sir Ivor	L Piggott	Red Alligator	B Fletcher
1969	Blakeney	E Johnson	Highland Wedding	E Harty
1970	Nijinsky	L Piggott	Gay Trip	P Taaffe
1971	Mill Reef	G Lewis	Specify	J Cook
1972	Roberto	L Piggott	Well To Do	G Thorner
1973	Morston	E Hide	Red Rum	B Fletcher
1974	Snow Knight	B Taylor	Red Rum	B Fletcher
1975	Grundy	P Eddery	L'Escargot	T Carberry
1976	Empery	L Piggott	Rag Trade	J Burke
1977	The Minstrel	L Piggott	Red Rum	T Stack
1978	Shirley Heights	G Starkey	Lucius	R Davies
1979	Troy	W Carson	Rubstic	M Barnes
1980	Henbit	W Carson	Ben Nevis	C Fenwick
1981	Shergar	W Swinburn	Aldaniti	R Champion
1982	Golden Fleece	P Eddery	Grittar	R Saunders
1983	Teenoso	L Piggott	Corbiere	B De Haan
1984	Secreto	C Roche	Hallo Dandy	N Doughty
1985	Slip Anchor	S Cauthen	Last Suspect	H Davies
1986	Shahrastani	W Swinburn	West Tip	R Dunwoody
1987	Reference Point	S Cauthen	Maori Venture	S Knight
1988	Kayhasi	R Cochrane	Rhyme 'n Reason	B Powell
1989	Nashwan	W Carson	Little Polveir	J Frost
1990	Quest for Fame	P Eddery	Mr Frisk	M Armytage
1991	Generous	A Munro	Seagram	N Hawke
1992	Dr Devious	J Reid	Party Politics	C Llewellyn
1993	Commander-in-Chief	MJ Kinane	*No race*	–
1994	Erhaab	W Carson	Minnehoma	R Dunwoody
1995	Lammtara	W Swinburn	Royal Athlete	J Titley
1996	Shaamit	M Hills	Rough Quest	M Fitzgerald
1997	Benny the Dip	W Ryan	Lord Gyllene	A Dobbin
1998	High Rise	O Peslier	Earth Summit	C Llewellyn
1999	Oath	K Fallon	Bobbyjo	P Carberry
2000	Sinndar	J Murtagh	Papillon	R Walsh

Golf Champions 1930–2000

	The Open	The Masters	Ryder Cup
1930	B Jones	–	–
1931	T Armour	–	USA
1932	G Sarazen	–	–
1933	D Shute	–	GB
1934	T Cotton	H Smith	–
1935	A Perry	G Sarazen	USA
1936	A Padgham	H Smith	–
1937	T Cotton	B Nelson	USA
1938	R Whitcombe	H Picard	–
1939	R Burton	R Guldahl	*Not held*
1940	*Not held*	J Demaret	
1941	*Not held*	C Wood	*Not held*
1942	*Not held*	B Nelson	–
1943	*Not held*	*Not held*	*Not held*
1944	*Not held*	*Not held*	–
1945	*Not held*	*Not held*	*Not held*
1946	S Snead	H Keiser	–
1947	F Daly	J Demaret	USA
1948	T Cotton	C Harmon	–
1949	B Locke	S Snead	USA
1950	B Locke	J Demaret	–
1951	M Faulkner	B Hogan	USA
1952	B Locke	S Snead	–
1953	B Hogan	B Hogan	USA
1954	P Thompson	S Snead	–
1955	P Thompson	C Middlecoff	USA
1956	P Thompson	J Burke Jnr	–
1957	B Locke	D Ford	GB
1958	P Thompson	A Palmer	–
1959	G Player	A Wall Jnr	USA
1960	K Nagle	A Palmer	–
1961	A Palmer	G Player	USA
1962	A Palmer	A Palmer	–
1963	R Charles	J Nicklaus	USA
1964	T Lema	A Palmer	–
1965	P Thompson	J Nicklaus	USA
1966	J Nicklaus	J Nicklaus	–

	The Open	The Masters	Ryder Cup
1967	R de Vicenzo	G Brewer	USA
1968	G Player	B Goalby	–
1969	A Jacklin	G Archer	Tie
1970	J Nicklaus	W Caspar	–
1971	L Trevino	C Coody	USA
1972	L Trevino	J Nicklaus	–
1973	T Weiskopf	T Aaron	USA
1974	G Player	G Player	–
1975	T Watson	J Nicklaus	USA
1976	J Miller	R Floyd	–
1977	T Watson	T Watson	USA
1978	J Nicklaus	G Player	–
1979	S Ballesteros	F Zoeller	USA
1980	T Watson	S Ballesteros	–
1981	W Rogers	T Watson	USA
1982	T Watson	C Stadler	–
1983	T Watson	S Ballesteros	USA
1984	S Ballesteros	B Crenshaw	–
1985	S Lyle	B Langer	Europe
1986	G Norman	J Nicklaus	–
1987	N Faldo	L Mize	Europe
1988	S Ballesteros	S Lyle	–
1989	M Calcavecchia	N Faldo	Tie
1990	N Faldo	N Faldo	–
1991	I Baker–Finch	I Woosnam	USA
1992	N Faldo	F Couples	–
1993	G Norman	B Langer	USA
1994	N Price	JM Olazabal	–
1995	J Daly	B Crenshaw	Europe
1996	T Lehman	N Faldo	–
1997	J Leonard	T Woods	Europe
1998	M O'Meara	M O'Meara	–
1999	P Lawrie	JM Olazabal	USA
2000	T Woods	VJ Singh	–

The Ryder Cup is contested every two years between Europe and USA. Prior to 1979 it was contested between GB and USA.

Wimbledon Champions 1930–2000

	Men	**Women**
1930	WT Tilden (USA)	HN Wills Moody (USA)
1931	SB Wood (USA)	C Aussem (Ger)
1932	HE Vines (USA)	HN Wills Moody (USA)
1933	JH Crawford (Aus)	HN Wills Moody (USA)
1934	FJ Perry (GB)	DE Round (GB)
1935	FJ Perry (GB)	HN Wills Moody (USA)
1936	FJ Perry (GB)	HH Jacobs (USA)
1937	JD Budge (USA)	DE Round (GB)
1938	JD Budge (USA)	HN Wills Moody (USA)
1939	RL Riggs (USA)	A Marble (USA)
1940	*Not held*	*Not held*
1941	*Not held*	*Not held*
1942	*Not held*	*Not held*
1943	*Not held*	*Not held*
1944	*Not held*	*Not held*
1945	*Not held*	*Not held*
1946	Y Petra (Fr)	PM Betz (USA)
1947	J Kramer (USA)	ME Osborne (USA)
1948	B Falkenburg (USA)	AL Brough (USA)
1949	T Schroeder (USA)	AL Brough (USA)
1950	B Patty (USA)	AL Brough (USA)
1951	D Savitt (USA)	DJ Hart (USA)
1952	F Sedgman (Aus)	M Connolly (USA)
1953	V Seixas (USA)	M Connolly (USA)
1954	J Drobny (Cze)	M Connolly (USA)
1955	MA Trabert (USA)	AL Brough (USA)
1956	LA Hoad (Aus)	SJ Fry (USA)
1957	LA Hoad (Aus)	A Gibson (USA)
1958	AJ Cooper (Aus)	A Gibson (USA)
1959	A Olmedo (Per)	ME Bueno (Bra)
1960	NA Fraser (Aus)	ME Bueno (Bra)
1961	RG Laver (Aus)	A Mortimer (GB)
1962	RG Laver (Aus)	K Hantze Susman (USA)
1963	CR McKinley (USA)	M Smith (Aus)
1964	RS Emerson (Aus)	ME Bueno (Bra)
1965	RS Emerson (Aus)	M Smith (Aus)
1966	M Santana (Sp)	BJ Moffitt King (USA)

	Men	Women
1967	JD Newcombe (Aus)	BJ King (USA)
1968	RG Laver (Aus)	BJ King (USA)
1969	RG Laver (Aus)	A Haydon Jones (GB)
1970	JD Newcombe (Aus)	M Smith Court (Aus)
1971	JD Newcombe (Aus)	EF Goolagong (Aus)
1972	SR Smith (USA)	BJ King (USA)
1973	J Kodes (Cze)	BJ King (USA)
1974	JS Connors (USA)	CM Evert (USA)
1975	AR Ashe (USA)	BJ King (USA)
1976	B Borg (Swe)	CM Evert (USA)
1977	B Borg (Swe)	SV Wade (GB)
1978	B Borg (Swe)	M Navratilova (Cze)
1979	B Borg (Swe)	M Navratilova (USA)
1980	B Borg (Swe)	EF Goolagong Cawley (Aus)
1981	JP McEnroe (USA)	CM Evert Lloyd (USA)
1982	JS Connors (USA)	M Navratilova (USA)
1983	JP McEnroe (USA)	M Navratilova (USA)
1984	JP McEnroe (USA)	M Navratilova (USA)
1985	B Becker (Ger)	M Navratilova (USA)
1986	B Becker (Ger)	M Navratilova (USA)
1987	P Cash (Aus)	M Navratilova (USA)
1988	S Edberg (Swe)	S Graf (Ger)
1989	B Becker (Ger)	S Graf (Ger)
1990	S Edberg (Swe)	M Navratilova (USA)
1991	M Stich (Ger)	S Graf (Ger)
1992	A Agassi (USA)	S Graf (Ger)
1993	P Sampras (USA)	S Graf (Ger)
1994	P Sampras (USA)	C Martinez (Sp)
1995	P Sampras (USA)	S Graf (Ger)
1996	R Krajicek (Ned)	S Graf (Ger)
1997	P Sampras (USA)	M Hingis (Swi)
1998	P Sampras (USA)	J Novotna (Cze)
1999	P Sampras (USA)	L Davenport (USA)
2000	P Sampras (USA)	V Williams (USA)

Formula 1 Motor Racing World Champions 1950–2000

Year	Driver	Country	Car
1950	Giuseppe Farina	Italy	Alfa Romeo
1951	Juan Manuel Fangio	Argentina	Alfa Romeo
1952	Alberto Ascari	Italy	Ferrari
1953	Alberto Ascari	Italy	Ferrari
1954	Juan Manuel Fangio	Argentina	Maserati/Mercedes
1955	Juan Manuel Fangio	Argentina	Mercedes-Benz
1956	Juan Manuel Fangio	Argentina	Lancia-Ferrari
1957	Juan Manuel Fangio	Argentina	Maserati
1958	Mike Hawthorn	UK	Ferrari
1959	Jack Brabham	Australia	Cooper-Climax
1960	Jack Brabham	Australia	Cooper-Climax
1961	Phil Hill	USA	Ferrari
1962	Graham Hill	UK	BRM
1963	Jim Clark	UK	Lotus-Climax
1964	John Surtees	UK	Ferrari
1965	Jim Clark	UK	Lotus-Climax
1966	Jack Brabham	Australia	Brabham-Repco
1967	Denny Hulme	New Zealand	Brabham-Repco
1968	Graham Hill	UK	Lotus-Ford
1969	Jackie Stewart	UK	Matra-Ford
1970	Jochen Rindt	Austria	Lotus-Ford
1971	Jackie Stewart	UK	Tyrrell-Ford
1972	Emerson Fittipaldi	Brazil	Lotus-Ford
1973	Jackie Stewart	UK	Tyrrell-Ford
1974	Emerson Fittipaldi	Brazil	McLaren-Ford
1975	Niki Lauda	Austria	Ferrari
1976	James Hunt	UK	McLaren-Ford
1977	Niki Lauda	Austria	Ferrari
1978	Mario Andretti	USA	Lotus-Ford
1979	Jody Scheckter	South Africa	Ferrari
1980	Alan Jones	Australia	Williams-Ford
1981	Nelson Piquet	Brazil	Brabham-Ford
1982	Keke Rosberg	Finland	Williams-Ford
1983	Nelson Piquet	Brazil	Brabham-BMW
1984	Niki Lauda	Austria	McLaren-TAG
1985	Alain Prost	France	McLaren-TAG
1986	Alain Prost	France	McLaren-TAG

Year	Driver	Country	Car
1987	Nelson Piquet	Brazil	Williams-Honda
1988	Ayrton Senna	Brazil	McLaren-Honda
1989	Alain Prost	France	McLaren-Honda
1990	Ayrton Senna	Brazil	McLaren-Honda
1991	Ayrton Senna	Brazil	McLaren-Honda
1992	Nigel Mansell	UK	Williams-Renault
1993	Alain Prost	France	Williams-Renault
1994	Michael Schumacher	Germany	Benetton-Ford
1995	Michael Schumacher	Germany	Benetton-Renault
1996	Damon Hill	UK	Williams-Renault
1997	Jacques Villeneuve	Canada	Williams-Renault
1998	Mika Hakkinen	Finland	McLaren-Mercedes
1999	Mika Hakkinen	Finland	McLaren-Mercedes
2000	Michael Schumacher	Germany	Ferrari

World Heavyweight Boxing Champions 1930–1980

12 June 1930	Max Schmeling
21 June 1932	Jack Sharkey
29 June 1933	Primo Carnera
14 June 1934	Max Baer
13 June 1935	James J. Braddock
22 June 1937	Joe Louis
27 September 1950	Ezzard Charles
18 July 1951	Jersey Joe Walcott
23 September 1952	Rocky Marciano
30 November 1956	Floyd Patterson
26 June 1959	Ingemar Johansson
20 June 1960	Floyd Patterson
25 September 1962	Sonny Liston

In 1963 a second boxing organisation, The World Boxing Council (WBC), was founded. Prior to this the sole authority was The World Boxing Association (WBA), originally founded as the National Boxing Association.

25 February 1964	Cassius Clay	WBA & WBC
19 June 1964	Muhammad Ali*	WBC
5 March 1965	Ernie Terrell	WBA
6 February 1967	Muhammad Ali**	WBA & WBC
4 March 1968	Joe Frazier	WBC
28 April 1968	Jimmy Ellis	WBA
16 February 1970	Joe Frazier	WBA & WBC
22 January 1973	George Foreman	WBA & WBC
30 October 1974	Muhammad Ali	WBA & WBC
15 February 1978	Leon Spinks	WBA & WBC
18 March 1978	Ken Norton	WBC
9 June 1978	Larry Holmes	WBC
15 September 1978	Muhammad Ali	WBA
20 October 1979	John Tate	WBA
31 March 1980	Mike Weaver	WBA

* Cassius Clay changed his name to Muhammad Ali

** In 1967 American boxing organisations stripped Muhammad Ali of his title upon his refusal to enter the US Army.

British Olympic Gold Medallists 1932–2000

Date	Venue	Discipline	Medalists
1932	Los Angeles	800m	Thomas Hampson
		50km walk	Thomas Green
		Rowing – coxless pairs	Team
		Rowing – coxless fours	Team
1936	Berlin	4 × 400m	Team
		50km walk	Harold Whitlock
		Rowing – double sculls	Team
		Yachting – 6m	Team
1948	London	Rowing – double sculls	Team
		Coxless pairs	Team
		Yachting – *Swallow*	David Bond
1952	Helsinki	Equestrian grand prix	Team
1956	Melbourne	3000m steeplechase	Chris Brasher
		100m backstroke	Judith Grinham
		Boxing – flyweight	Terence Spinks
		Boxing – lightweight	Richard McTaggart
		Fencing – foil	Gillian Sheen
		Equestrian – 3-day event	Team
		Equestrian – dressage	Team
1960	Rome	50km walk	Donald Thompson
		200m breaststroke	Anita Lonsbrough
1964	Tokyo	800m	Ann Packer
		Long jump	Mary Rand
		Long jump	Lynn Davies
		20km walk	Kenneth Matthews
1968	Mexico	400m hurdles	David Hemery
		Boxing – middleweight	Chris Finnegan
		Shooting – clay pigeon	John Robert Braithwaite
		Yachting – *Flying Dutchman*	Team
		Equestrian 3-day event	Team

Date	Venue	Discipline	Medalists
1972	Munich	Pentathlon	Mary Peters
		Yachting – *Flying Dutchman*	Team
		Equestrian 3-day event	Richard Meade
		Equestrian 3-day event	Team
1976	Montreal	200m breaststroke	David Wilkie
		Modern pentathlon	Team
		Yachting – *Tornado*	Team
1980	Moscow	100m	Allan Wells
		800m	Steve Ovett
		1500m	Sebastian Coe
		Decathlon	Daley Thompson
		100m breaststroke	Duncan Goodhew
1984	Los Angeles	1500m	Sebastian Coe
		Decathlon	Daley Thompson
		Javelin	Tessa Sanderson
		Rowing – coxed fours	Team
		Shooting – small bore rifle	Malcolm Cooper
1988	Seoul	100m Breaststroke	Adrian Moorhouse
		Shooting – small bore rifle	Malcolm Cooper
		Rowing – coxless pairs	Team
		Yachting – *Star*	Team
		Hockey	Team
1992	Barcelona	100m	Linford Christie
		400m hurdles	Sally Gunnell
		Rowing – coxed pairs	Team
		Rowing – coxless pairs	Team
		Cycling – 4,000m pursuit	Chris Boardman
1996	Atlanta	Rowing – coxless pairs	Team
2000	Sydney	Triple jump	Jonathan Edwards
		Modern pentathlon	Stephanie Cook
		Heptathlon	Denise Lewis
		Boxing – super heavyweight	Audley Harrison

Date	Venue	Discipline	Medalists
2000 (cont.)		Cycling – 1km sprint	Jason Queally
		Rowing – coxed eight	Team
		Rowing – coxless fours	Team
		Sailing – *Europe Dinghy*	Shirley Robertson
		Sailing – *Finn*	Iain Percy
		Sailing – *Laser*	Ben Ainslie
		Shooting – double trap	Richard Faulds

Appendix 2

A Few of My Favourite Things

The object of this section is to get you thinking about your own life. For example, your favourite songs might be related to special times and evoke powerful memories.

You can also use the lists as a game. For example, how many of your mother's top ten songs or films could you name? I did the same with my wife and only came up with three.... could do better! With these lists of favourites, you might like to write why they are so special and any associated memories. If you are trying to encourage your parents to write, this section might be a useful appetiser, if only to prove to them how much they can remember and how interesting their lives are to others.

The lists include the most influential people in your life, both those you have known and those you have admired from afar – not people you've met (or maybe only briefly). Depending on how open you want to be, you might also like to review your life so far – your successes, lessons learned and what you might do differently were you to have your time again. Space has been left at the back for such a purpose or anything else you would like to record.

Five people who have most influenced your life

These need not necessarily be the obvious ones like parents (although they could be included), but those who have believed in you and who have helped shape the course of your life, like a teacher, a friend, a colleague etc. You might like to record how they have influenced the course of your life.

1 . . . .

2 . . . .

3 . . . .

4 . . . .

5 . . . .

Five people admired from afar

These could be famous or otherwise – not people you've met (or maybe only briefly). Include what you most admire about them.

1 . . . .

2 . . . .

3 . . . .

4 . . . .

5 . . . .

Favourite Films

1 . . . .

2 . . . .

3 . . . .

4 . . . .

5 . . . .

6 . . . .

7 . . . .

8 . . . .

9 . . . .

10 . . . .

Favourite Actors and Actresses

You might like to include whether you have met any of these in person.

1 . . . .

2 . . . .

3 . . . .

4 . . . .

5 . . . . ▶

Favourite Actors and Actresses (continued)

6 . . . .

7 . . . .

8 . . . .

9 . . . .

10 . . . .

Favourite Shows, Plays, Musicals, Ballets etc

1 . . . .

2 . . . .

3 . . . .

4 . . . .

5 . . . .

6 . . . .

7 . . . .

8 . . . .

9 . . . .

10 . . . .

Favourite Books

1 . . . .

2 . . . .

3 . . . .

4 . . . .

5 . . . .

6 . . . .

7 . . . .

8 . . . .

9 . . . .

10 . . . .

Favourite Authors

1 . . . .

2 . . . .

3 . . . .

4 . . . .

5 . . . .

6 . . . . ▶

Favourite Authors (continued)

7 . . . .

8 . . . .

9 . . . .

10 . . . .

Favourite Songs

1 . . . .

2 . . . .

3 . . . .

4 . . . .

5 . . . .

6 . . . .

7 . . . .

8 . . . .

9 . . . .

10 . . . .

Favourite Singers, Musicians, Bands, Orchestras etc

1 . . . .

2 . . . .

3 . . . .

4 . . . .

5 . . . .

6 . . . .

7 . . . .

8 . . . .

9 . . . .

10 . . . .

Favourite Food, Meals and Restaurants

Perhaps including your own recipes.

1 . . . .

2 . . . .

3 . . . .

4 . . . .

5 . . . .

Favourite Food, Meals and Restaurants (continued)

6 . . . .

7 . . . .

8 . . . .

9 . . . .

10 . . . .

Sporting Highs… and Lows (Your Own)

1 . . . .

2 . . . .

3 . . . .

4 . . . .

5 . . . .

6 . . . .

7 . . . .

8 . . . .

9 . . . .

10 . . . .

Memorable Sporting Moments You Have Witnessed

1 . . . .

2 . . . .

3 . . . .

4 . . . .

5 . . . .

6 . . . .

7 . . . .

8 . . . .

9 . . . .

10 . . . .

Favourite countries visited

1 . . . .

2 . . . .

3 . . . .

4 . . . .

5 . . . .

6 . . . . ▶

Favourite countries visited (continued)

7 . . . .

8 . . . .

9 . . . .

10 . . . .

Ambitions Achieved

1 . . . .

2 . . . .

3 . . . .

4 . . . .

5 . . . .

6 . . . .

7 . . . .

8 . . . .

9 . . . .

10 . . . .

Ambitions Outstanding

1 . . . .

2 . . . .

3 . . . .

4 . . . .

5 . . . .

6 . . . .

7 . . . .

8 . . . .

9 . . . .

10 . . . .

Happiest Times of Your Life

1 . . . .

2 . . . .

3 . . . .

4 . . . .

5 . . . .

6 . . . . ▶

Happiest Times of Your Life (continued)

7 . . . .

8 . . . .

9 . . . .

10 . . . .

Most Satisfying Achievements

1 . . . .

2 . . . .

3 . . . .

4 . . . .

5 . . . .

6 . . . .

7 . . . .

8 . . . .

9 . . . .

10 . . . .

Turning Points in Your Life

1 ....

2 ....

3 ....

4 ....

5 ....

6 ....

7 ....

8 ....

9 ....

10 ....

Your Idea of a Perfect Day

1 ....

2 ....

3 ....

4 ....

5 ....

6 .... ▶

Your Idea of a Perfect Day (continued)

7 . . . .

8 . . . .

9 . . . .

10 . . . .

Notes

. . . .

. . . .

. . . .

. . . .

. . . .

. . . .

. . . .

. . . .

. . . .

. . . .

. . . .

Glossary

Advance. A sum paid to the author in advance of publication of a book.

Agent. See **literary agent**.

Artistic Licence. A term used for the author to embellish the writing, particularly with regard to stretching the truth.

Autobiography. A life story written by the person concerned.

Biography. A life story researched and written by someone other than the subject of the book. The term is also often used generically to refer to both biographies and autobiographies.

Cliffhanger. A writing technique found at the end of a chapter or even a book, designed to keep the reader wanting more.

Copyright. The exclusive right to written, electronic or oral material. The ownership rests with the author unless legally assigned to a third party.

Draft. Any early version of the manuscript.

Edit. To revise a manuscript looking for mistakes, repetitions, ambiguities, inconsistencies and omissions, to improve the work.

Flashback. A writing technique where the story jumps back in time. Useful for dramatic effect, or to help overcome difficulties with the chronology, especially in a book covering the life of more than one person.

House style. A set of guidelines regarding the use of punctuation, numbering systems etc. to ensure consistency throughout a work.

ISBN. International Standard Book Number, a unique ten-digit reference number allocated by Nielsen Book Data to identify and aid the reordering of published books.

Ghostwriter. A third party who writes about the person who is the subject of the book, usually with the subject's assistance, but not necessarily so in the case of an unauthorised biography. Any credit given to the ghostwriter is usually couched in such words as 'with assistance from . . .'

GSM. Grams per square metre – the weight system applied to paper.

Internet. Global computer network with a standard addressing system.

Libel. Writing which damages a person's reputation or livelihood.

Life story. Autobiography or biography.

Literary agent. A person who acts on behalf of the author in dealings with the publisher – both offering the work and negotiating contracts. Usually receiving a commission in the order of 10–15% from what the author receives, the agent is paid by results.

Manuscript. The handwritten, typed or word processed material which represents work in progress prior to a book being produced.

Memoir. An autobiography, usually in the form of selected anecdotes rather than a detailed, chronological life story.

Oral history. Recording the spoken word on tape.

Pagination. The laying out of a page with text and/or pictures in preparation for the final book.

Proofread. To review the manuscript thoroughly, usually just prior to printing, to eliminate mistakes and inconsistencies.

Vanity publishing. A term applied when an author pays to have a book published.

Web page. A private text and graphical 'page' on the Internet.

Useful Addresses

Age Exchange
The Reminiscence Centre, 11 Blackheath Village, London SE3 9LA.
Tel: (020) 8318 9105
Website: *www.age-exchange.org.uk*

Association of Personal Historians
Website: *www.personalhistorians.org*

Bound Biographies Limited
Heyford Park House, Heyford Park, Bicester, Oxfordshire OX25 5HD
Tel: 01869 232911.
Website: *www.boundbiographies.com*
email: *office@boundbiographies.com*

British Library Newspapers
Colindale Avenue, London NW9 5HE.
Tel: (020) 7412 7353.
Website: *www.bl.uk/services/reading/newsprepare.html*

Directory of Writers' Circles,
39 Lincoln Way, Harlington, Beds LU5 6NG.
Tel: 01525 873197.
Website: *www.writers-circles.com*

Friends Reunited.
Website: *www.friendsreunited.com*

The Living Archive
The Old Bath House, 205 Stratford Road, Wolverton,
Milton Keynes, Bucks MK12 5RL.
Tel: 01908 322568
Website: *www.livingarchive.org.uk*

Museum of Brands, Packaging and Advertising,
2 Colville Mews, Lonsdale Road, Notting Hill, London W11 2AR.
Tel: 0207 908 0880.
Website: *www.museumofbrands.com*

National Association of Writers' Groups,
The Arts Centre, Biddick Lane, Washington, Tyne & Wear
NE38 2AB.
Tel: 01262 609228.
Website: *www.nawg.co.uk*

Nielsen Book Data
ISBN Agency, 3rd Floor, Midas House, 62 Goldsworth Road,
Woking, Surrey GU21 6LQ
Tel: 0870 777 8710.
Website: *www.isbn.nielsenbookdata.co.uk*

The Oral History Society
c/o Department of History, University of Essex, Colchester
CO4 3SQ
Tel: (020) 7412 7405
Website: *www.ohs.org.uk*

The Royal British Legion, 48 Pall Mall, London SW1Y 5JY.
Tel: (020) 7973 7200
Website: *www.britishlegion.org.uk*

The Society of Authors
84 Drayton Gardens, London SW10 9SB.
Tel: (020) 7373 6642
Website: *www.societyofauthors.org*

U3A (University of the Third Age)
National Office: The Third Age Trust,
The Old Municipal Buildings, 19 East Street, Kent BR1 1QE
Tel: 020 8466 6139
Website: *www.u3a.org.uk*

The national office will be happy to provide details of local contacts, as will your local library.

Other reference materials

British Newspaper Library – see above

Oral History Society – see above

Nostalgia Museums

Past Times Shops

Videos/DVDs – *A Year to Remember* series (Telstar Video Entertainment)

The 1940s House (Wall to Wall Television for Channel 4)

Typing and proofreading services

Recommendations can usually be provided by writers' groups and writers' circles (see above), libraries and typing colleges. Advertisements can also be found in various writing magazines.

Further Reading

Books

Chronicle of the 20th Century, Dorling Kindersley.
Creative Writing, Adèle Ramet, How to Books.
Starting to Write, Marina and Deborah Oliver, How To Books.
The 1940s House, Juliet Gardiner, Channel 4 Books.
The Writer's Handbook, Macmillan.
Times of Our Lives, Michael Oke, How To Books.
Writers' and Artists' Yearbook, A. & C. Black.
Writing for Publication, Chriss McCallum, How To Books.

Magazines

Ancestors
PO Box 38, Richmond TW9 4AJ.
Tel: 020 8392 5370
Website: *www.ancestorsmagazine.co.uk*

BBC Who Do You Think You Are?
Tower House, Fairfax Street, Bristol BS1 3BN.
Tel: 0117 927 9009
Website: *www.bbcwhodoyouthinkyouare.com*

Best of British, Church Lane Publishing Ltd, Bank Chambers,
27a Market Place, Market Deeping, Lincolnshire PE6 8EA.
Tel: 01778 342814.
Website: *www.bestofbritishmag.co.uk*

Choice First Floor, 2 King Street, Peterborough, PE1 1LT.
Tel: 01733 555123
Website: *www.choicemag.co.uk*

Evergreen, PO BOX 52, Cheltenham, Gloucestershire GL50 1YQ.
Tel: 01242 537900.
Website: *www.evergreenmagazine.co.uk*

Family Tree, 61 Great Whyte, Ramsey, Huntingdon,
Cambridgeshire, PE26 1HJ.
Tel: 08707 662272
Website: *www.family-tree.co.uk*

The Overseas Pensioner, 138 High Street, Tonbridge, Kent
TN9 1AX. Tel: 01732 363836.
Website: *www.ospa.org.uk/journal.asp*

Saga, Saga Publishing Ltd, The Saga Building, Middelburg
Square, Folkestone, Kent CT20 1AZ.
Tel: 01303 771111.
Website: *www.saga.co.uk/saga-magazine*

Writers' Forum
Select Publisher Services Ltd, P.O. Box 6337, Bournemouth
BH9 1EH.
Tel: 01202 586848
Website: *www.writers-forum.com*

Writers' News and Writing Magazine, 5th Floor,
31–32 Park Row, Leeds LS1 5JD.
Tel: (0113) 200 2929.
Website: *www.writersnews.co.uk*

Yours, Apex House, Oundle Road, Peterborough, PE2 9NP.
Tel: 01733 898100.
Website: *www.yours.co.uk*

Index

Michael Oke and his colleagues assist in the writing of private life stories. Via a series of home visits, or by correspondence, guidance and encouragement is provided for those looking to write for family, friends and for the sheer fun of it.

Editing and production services are also offered to those who have already written a manuscript.

Eitherway, the end result is a few high-quality, leather-bound volumes, including photographs. Low runs of smaller hardback and paperback books can also be provided.

Name:

Address:

Phone:

Bound Biographies Ltd, 23 Heyford Park House
Heyford Park, Bicester, Oxon OX25 5HD
Telephone: 01869 232911
www.boundbiographies.com

--- ✄ ---

Michael Oke and his colleagues assist in the writing of private life stories. Via a series of home visits, or by correspondence, guidance and encouragement is provided for those looking to write for family, friends and for the sheer fun of it.

Editing and production services are also offered to those who have already written a manuscript.

Eitherway, the end result is a few high-quality, leather-bound volumes, including photographs. Low runs of smaller hardback and paperback books can also be provided.

Name:

Address:

Phone:

Bound Biographies Ltd, 23 Heyford Park House
Heyford Park, Bicester, Oxon OX25 5HD
Telephone: 01869 232911
www.boundbiographies.com